IT DEPENDS WHAT YOU MEAN

An Improvisation for the Glockenspiel

IT DEPENDS WHAT YOU MEAN

An Improvisation for the Glockenspiel

BY

JAMES BRIDIE

CONSTABLE AND COMPANY LTD.
LONDON

LONDON

PUBLISHED BY

Constable and Company Ltd.

10-12 ORANGE STREET, W.C. 2.

•

INDIA

Longmans, Green and Company Ltd.

BOMBAY   CALCUTTA   MADRAS

•

CANADA

Longmans, Green and Company

TORONTO

First Published 1948

Printed in Great Britain by
W. & J. Mackay and Co., Ltd., Chatham

PERSONS IN THE PLAY

ANGELA PROUT, B.A.

THE REV. WILLIAM PARIS, C.F.

GEORGE PROUT, R.O.I.

JAMES MUTCH, D.LITT.

PTE. JESSIE KILLIGREW, A.T.S.

VISCOUNTESS DODD, D.B.E.

JOE BYRES, M.P.

HECTOR MACADAM, M.D., F.R.C.S.ED.

PTE. WALTER GEIKIE, R.A.S.C.

TIME :   1942.

PLACE :   North Britain.

SCENES :   A Studio and an Army Recreation Hut.

NOTE :—*The Characters in this Play are not intended to represent any existing individuals.*

IT DEPENDS WHAT YOU MEAN

ACT I

SCENE :—*A small bare, but untidy, Studio in a small country town. The Stage is empty. A car is heard braking fiercely just outside, and immediately after a knocker is heard banging at the door.*

ANGELA PROUT ENTERS *through a curtained doorway, crosses the stage and opens the door. She is a slatternly but not unattractive woman of about thirty-five with an extremely intelligent face. She admits a* CLERGYMAN *in Battle Dress.*

ANGELA. Oh, do come in ; I am sorry to have kept you waiting, but this is an artist's house, and you know what that means.

PADRE. Oh yes, thank you. It's quite all right.

ANGELA. Won't you sit down ?

PADRE. Thank you, yes, rather.

[HE *sits.*

A very jolly place you have here, Mrs. Prout.

ANGELA. Oh, do you think so ? It seems to me a dreary little hovel. Thank God my husband's an artist and I'm not supposed to keep it clean, though mind you, I've searched three counties for a charwoman. I think the race must be extinct. Such a pity. I didn't exactly love them in the old days, but absence does make the heart grow fonder, doesn't it, Mr.——I mean Captain, of course.

PADRE. Oh, Mr.'s quite all right. I'm a padre, as a matter of fact. Paris is the name.

ANGELA. Oh, I'm so sorry, but one never knows these days, does one ? I got quite a shock when our doctor in Chelsea suddenly turned up looking the perfect man of blood. Such a kind little chap he was too. An osteopath

[7]

really, though he was a proper doctor as well. He's a major now—eating raw beefsteaks and using terrible language. Now I'll get you some tea. George and Jimmy Mutch are arguing about spring onions and neither of them knows a thing about spring onions. I'll shout for them. (*Goes to the window.*)

PADRE. Oh no, really, please, you mustn't bother.

ANGELA. Don't you want tea ?

PADRE. Well, persons of my cloth have the name of being addicts, haven't they ?

ANGELA. That's all right then. That's settled. Besides, we were having it anyhow. (*Shouting through the window.*) Georgie ! Come in ; we've got a visitor.

GEORGE (*without*). Oh hell !

ANGELA. And it's tea-time.

GEORGE (*without*). Blast !

ANGELA. I'm so sorry there's no whisky. Do you find that tea is very bad for your patients' tempers ?

PADRE. Patients ?

ANGELA. Oh, I forgot, you're not a doctor, but George is much easier to live with when there is plenty of whisky in the house, and tea seems to have just the opposite effect. I say, what about your driver ?

PADRE. Well, if you would be so extraordinarily kind I'll take out a cup.

ANGELA. Is it a he, or a she ?

PADRE. It's a she.

ANGELA. Is she good looking ?

PADRE. Well—yes, I suppose so, rather.

ANGELA. Bring her in then. George is terribly fond of pretty girls.

PADRE. Really ? Do you mind ? She's rather good fun. Rather a character in her way.

ANGELA. Right-ho then. Bring her in. I'll go and fetch the tea.

[EXIT ANGELA. PADRE *opens the door and calls.*

PADRE.   Jessie!   Will you come in, please?   Mrs. Prout is going to give us a cup of tea.

JESSIE (*without*).   Oh, hoorray!

[ENTER PROUT *and* MUTCH.   THEY *almost bump into the* PADRE.

PROUT.   Hello!

PADRE.   Hello!

PROUT.   I say, look here, I'm terribly sorry.   We can't billet anybody here.   The place isn't fit to keep a pig in.   Professor Mutch here has much or less to sleep in the scullery.

PADRE.   That's all right.   I'm not the Billeting Officer.   I'm not an officer at all actually.   I'm only a padre.

PROUT.   Only a padre?   What an appalling thing to say.   A direct representative of the Almighty isn't *only* anything.   Is he, Jimmy?

MUTCH.   Well, I mean to say, after all. . . .   Humility, I mean.   Isn't it one of the apostolic virtues?

PADRE (*laughing*).   Ha, ha!   Well, I suppose it ought to be, oughtn't it?   Oh, there you are, Jessie.

[ENTER *a very smart member of the* A.T.S. SHE *is at her ease, but a little on guard.*

This is my driver, Private Killigrew.   Mrs. Prout very kindly said she might come in for a cup of tea.

PROUT.   Naturally, yes, of course.   Very pleased.   How do you do?

JESSIE.   How do you do?

PADRE.   You're the celebrated Professor Mutch, aren't you?

MUTCH.   Well, as a matter of fact, yes.

PADRE.   I thought I recognised you from your photographs. Private Killigrew, this is Professor Mutch.

JESSIE.   How do you do?

MUTCH.   How do you do?

PADRE.   And you're Mr. Prout, aren't you?

PROUT.   Yes.

PADRE.   I'm Paris.

PROUT. Good. Now we know each other. And now I hope that draggle-tailed harridan, the wife of my bosom, is hurrying up with the tea.

PADRE. I do wish she wouldn't bother. As a matter of fact I only called in for a minute. I wanted to ask you to do us a great favour.

PROUT. Who's us? Sit down, Miss What's-your-name.

[MUTCH *gets a chair for* JESSIE. *All sit.*

Who's us?

PADRE. Well, the troops, you see.

PROUT. Have you a cigarette, Padre?

PADRE. I only learned last night that we had three such celebrated people in the neighbourhood and the O.C. and I decided to cash in on it.

PROUT. Got a match?

PADRE. I'm sorry, I don't smoke. Where was I? The Welfare Officer's in hospital you see, and I'm sort of stooging for him. I wonder if you'd care to take part in the Brains Trust we're holding in the Canteen next week?

PROUT. Brains Trust? But I've got no brains and Jimmy here is practically an imbecile. He's no worse than his stupider sort of neighbour in ordinary conversation, but wait till you see him before an audience.

PADRE. Oh come, come, come, come, come, come, come. (To Mutch) I'm afraid our friend is a bit of a legpuller, isn't he?

PROUT. I'm nothing of the sort.

MUTCH. You are in a way, old boy. You've a sadistic streak in you.

PROUT. But I've never pulled anyone's leg in my life. Why should I? Where is that infernal woman? I want my tea. At least I don't want it, but I need it. Angela!

ANGELA (*without*). Coming, coming.

[ENTER ANGELA *carrying a tray with tea things. With the rather fussy assistance of the* PADRE *she puts it down on a low table and the tea-party starts.*

MUTCH. I have noticed that sculptors, and people generally who make things with their hands, are very often deficient in self-criticism.

ANGELA. Can you take goat's milk, Padre?

PADRE. Yes, thanks. Thanks very much.

MUTCH. I don't mean they don't criticise themselves. They do.

ANGELA. We've no sugar, I'm sorry, but we are rather proud of our goat's milk.

MUTCH. But it is usually a very inexpert sort of criticism.

PADRE. Do you mind if I use my saccharine? Would anyone else like some?

ANGELA. I'm sure they would.

PROUT. Thanks very much.

JESSIE. Yes, thank you.

MUTCH. Over their work I mean.

PADRE. There you are. Help yourselves.

PROUT. Thank you very much.

MUTCH. I don't mean after it's completed and, so to speak, away from them. A picture or a piece of sculpture is budded off from the artist.

ANGELA. Did you know we had a nanny goat?

PADRE. No, really?

MUTCH. It's like that sea water creature—I forget it's name.

ANGELA. She's called Lady Cabstanleigh, after Beachcomber. She's got the same kind of expression in her eyes.

MUTCH. It grows its young like little buds from the stalk——

PADRE. Now you come and sit here, Mrs. Prout.

ANGELA. Bring that chair down.

MUTCH. They grow their young on a kind of stalk, but the stalk breaks off and the infants float away and become separate entities. It's only when the artist's work has budded off and floated away and grown up a bit that the artist is really fit to give any opinion about it at all. It's then an entity like himself and not part of himself, if you see what I mean.

ANGELA. Yes, dear Jimmy, we see what you mean. (*To* JESSIE.) I suppose the boys at the camp get plenty of sugar?

JESSIE. Yes.

PADRE. I tell the boys they don't know they're born, they get lashings of sugar.

ANGELA. The lucky fellows!

PROUT. What do you mean by " lucky "? I had a year of the army before they chucked me out and I never went through such indiluted hell since I was at school.

ANGELA. I often think——

PROUT. Nonsense.

ANGELA. My dear George, I am accustomed to the peculiar Chesterfieldian grace of your interjections, but I wonder what Mr. Paris will think of us.

PROUT. Who's Mr. Paris?

ANGELA. This is Mr. Paris.

PROUT. Oh, I know what he thinks of us. He thinks we're a ready-made Brains Trust.

ANGELA. Brains Trust?

PADRE. Yes. In point of fact, I called to see whether you and Mr. Prout and the Professor would help us. I hate the name Brains Trust, but the troops always call it that and they love it. Will you help us?

ANGELA. Yes, of course we will. What fun! Is Professor Joad coming?

MUTCH. My God!

PADRE. No. We're relying on what I may call local talent. I'd better tell you who the other members are. There's the local doctor, he's a very clever man. He won all sorts of medals at Edinburgh. Then, of course, there's Lady Dodd.

PROUT. Why " of course "?

PADRE. Well, she's a very busy woman, and it was very nice of her to jump at the suggestion—and she's very popular with the troops. And then there's Mr. Byres.

PROUT. Who's he?

PADRE. He's the Member of Parliament for the county. Of course he's a Labour Member, but I don't think we should allow that to weigh with us in war-time, do you ? I've told him he mustn't talk politics.

PROUT. Why shouldn't he ? If he's a Labour Member politics are the only things under heaven that he knows any-thing about. Are you going to forbid me to talk about painting ? Aren't you going to allow Angela to talk about poetry ? Aren't you going to talk about religion ?

PADRE. Well, I'm not as a matter of fact. You and Mrs. Prout can talk about what you like. But one has to be so careful, hasn't one ? We don't want to hurt anyone's feelings.

PROUT. That's why nobody goes to church nowadays. You don't want to hurt anyone's feelings. You can't say, "It's a fine day" without hurting somebody's feelings ; so you've got to talk meaningless gibberish.

ANGELA. Darling, the Padre is not talking meaningless gibberish.

PROUT. I know. But the result is that he's hurt my feelings very severely.

PADRE. Oh, have I ? I hope not.

PROUT (*walking up and down*). I'm a workman—a plain man of my hands. But I'm the best workman in my own line of business in the British Islands ; and I'm to be made a cock-shy with a row of other Aunt Sallies, including my Lady Dodd, God bless her, to keep the British soldier out of the public-house where he'd be much better employed. Do you realise, sir, that I take the profession of Michael Angelo and Velasquez with some seriousness ?

PADRE. Of course I realise that. I take my own humble profession with some seriousness also. But that has nothing to do with the point. Even Michael Angelo could bring him-self now and again to answer a polite question or two. And that's all I'm asking you to do. You'll persuade him, won't you, Mrs. Prout ?

ANGELA. I can't persuade him to do anything—even to change his underclothing.

MUTCH. I'll persuade him.

PADRE. Will you ?

B   [13]

MUTCH. Well, I don't know whether you would exactly call it persuasion. But if I hear him standing on his dignity as an artist something will impel me to lick the living soul-case out of him.

PADRE. Dear me !

ANGELA. He could, you know. He used to box for his university. And George is a terrible physical coward. He won't even milk Lady Cabstanleigh because he's afraid she might butt him.

PROUT. Of course if you wish to lay bare the most secret corners of our private life to every Tom, Dick and Harry who happens to drop in. . . .

ANGELA. Nonsense, George. Mr. Paris and Miss What's-her-name aren't Tom, Dick and Harry. Besides you said yourself that it would be a better world if we all told the truth about ourselves.

PROUT. There you go again. I told you that in confidence.

ANGELA. That's another thing about him, Mr. Paris. He talks platitudes in confidence.

PROUT. All right, let's take all our clothes off. Show him your appendix scar, Angela, won't you ? And I've got a most entertaining birth mark. I don't think there's anything particularly interesting about Jimmy—except that he looks damned funny in the buff.

MUTCH. Really, George. But come along, let's get cracking. We're wasting time. The Padre wants to know all about us.

ANGELA (to JESSIE). What a lovely ring you're wearing.

JESSIE. We're not supposed to wear them when we're in uniform, but the Padre lets me wear it when I'm driving him.

ANGELA. It's a beauty.

JESSIE. Yes, isn't it ? I wouldn't have got a ring like this, only Walter—that's my boy-friend—saved an old pawn-broker from getting beaten up in the black-out. I don't know how he did it. He's like your old man, he's not much of a scrapper; but he says he remembered one or two dirty tricks from the unarmed combat course. He wouldn't tell me what they were. Said they weren't fit for a lady to hear.

[14]

ANGELA. Still, you must be very proud of him.

JESSIE. Oh, I don't know.

ANGELA. You don't know! He comes back to you like a privateering captain and throws the spoils of the Indies into your lap and you say you don't know!

JESSIE. Well, I don't, and that's the truth. You see, he hasn't got much of an education.

MUTCH. He seems to have picked up one or two quite valuable pieces of information in his physical training class. After all, that's what education does, doesn't it? Or ought to do. It fits one to meet emergencies.

JESSIE. Oh *that* kind of education! He's got plenty of that, and he's a good mechanic too. But that's not what I call education.

MUTCH. What do you call education?

JESSIE. How should I know? I never had any.

ANGELA. Then what do you mean?

JESSIE. Oh, I don't know. Being able to talk about things like you three here and the Padre and that. The way I look at it, Walter can only talk about what I look like, and his blooming engines and that. That's all right in its way, but it's going to spread out a bit thin over thirty or forty years. And education makes you understand people. Walter doesn't understand me a bit. He says so himself.

ANGELA. But surely if you're both at the same level of education. . . .

JESSIE. Well, it seems to me that if you are neither of you is any better off. I think people should marry to better themselves, don't you? Or anyway at least one of them ought to be better off.

ANGELA. Dear me! That is very materialistic of you. Almost commercial. What about falling in love?

JESSIE. I don't know so much about that. I mean falling in love's very nice and all that, but where's your guarantee that both of them are going to be in love till death doth them part? It's taking a big risk.

ANGELA. But if a thing's worth doing it is worth taking a big risk for it.

JESSIE. That's what my father used to say, and mother and me had to whip round the neighbours to pay for his funeral. You see where I come from in Civvy Street we only talk about things. We don't talk about what they're all about. They go on happening and they don't seem to mean anything, somehow. That's why I sometimes think I'd like to marry a man with brains and spend the rest of my life trying to find out what it all means.

ANGELA. I wouldn't do that if I were you.

JESSIE. But I want to know, you see.

PADRE, Well, well, well, we can thrash that out on Friday.

ANGELA. On Friday, is it?

PADRE. Yes, next Friday. I'm sorry it's such short notice, but may I take it that you will come?

ANGELA. But of course we'll come. We are boring each other stiff here, and it will be a great treat to bore somebody else for a change.

MUTCH. I don't know whether I shall be here next Friday. I only came down for a week-end and I've been here for ten days.

ANGELA. You can go away on Saturday, so it's all arranged.

PADRE. Splendid, splendid. We'll send a car for you at half past seven and that will give you time to have a glass of South African sherry in the Mess before we go round to the Recreation Hut. I'm certain that you will enjoy it and I know that the troops will be immensely honoured.

[HE *gets up.*

Now I must get back. Oh, my goodness, my saccharine! (*Picks up box.*) Thank you so much for the tea, Mrs. Prout. We shall all look forward to a most interesting evening.

ANGELA. I suppose we'll have to answer a lot of terrifying questions?

JESSIE. I shall ask one.

MUTCH. Oh, will you? What will you ask?

PADRE. That's not fair. You mustn't know the questions beforehand.

ANGELA (*to* JESSIE). You must come round and have tea again. You can bring any of the girls who would like to come, and Walter too if you like.

JESSIE. If you don't mind I would rather come myself.

PADRE. Now we must get cracking. *Au revoir.*

OMNES. Goody-bye. Good-afternoon.

ANGELA (*going out*). I'm afraid we've not been very hospitable to the camp people, but then we're not very hospitable people.

PADRE (*going out*). Oh, indeed you are.

[EXEUNT ANGELA, JESSIE *and* PADRE

PROUT. I say, Jimmy.

MUTCH. Yes, George?

PROUT. That was an odd thing you said.

MUTCH. What?

PROUT. You said you'd give me a hammering if I didn't go. Do you know that I suddenly believed you?

MUTCH. Oh, well, I mean to say, good gracious me!

PROUT. Do you remember my first day at school?

MUTCH. Well, no, not exactly.

PROUT. My old man put me in your charge, and you took over quite solemnly, and he gave you half-a-sovereign. Then you took me into your stinking little cubby-hole and do you remember what you said?

MUTCH. No. No, I don't.

PROUT. You said to me—" You were always a conceited little bastard, and I don't like the way you walk on your heels, or, indeed, anything about you. But I promised your guv'nor I'd do my best for you, and I will . . . I'm going to knock some of the bloody side out of you to save the beaks and the other fellows the trouble." Then you gave me the hammering of my life. You sadistic little swine that you were. . . . I had exactly the same feeling a moment ago. It was astonishing and most unpleasant.

[17]

MUTCH. Well, I hope it did you no harm. I remember now you *were* a cocky little brute. I probably did you a damned good turn.

PROUT. I spent the next fortnight thinking out ways of killing you. But it never came to anything.

MUTCH. Not yet, eh?

PROUT. Not yet, but I don't suppose I ever will kill you ; you amuse me and Angela likes you—I can't think why.

MUTCH. Probably because I'm not rude to her in public.

PROUT. Rude to her? In public? Me? Good Gubbins. Pull yourself together, Jimmy. Angela and I are terrific pals.

MUTCH. I know that.

PROUT. I think in the whole circle of my acquaintance we're the only happy couple who are legally married. We're terrific pals. I don't know what I should do without her, blast her ! Where is she, by the way?

MUTCH. She must have gone down to the gate with the Padre.

PROUT. Trying to fascinate him, I suppose. Poor old devil, that's not her line of country. I think that's probably why I like her so much—she's so completely unfascinating. I'd hate to be married to one of these disturbing women. They're as selfish as hell, and full of unscrupulous tricks. But Angy's not like that. She's no Helen of Troy, and I know it, and she knows it, and she knows I know it. And so we get on like a house on fire.

MUTCH. Oh, you do, do you? I mean, do you?

PROUT. Well, don't we? You know as well as anybody that we do—damn it.

MUTCH. Yes, I suppose you do. Yes, oh yes, rather, of course, yes. Now, about onions. I mean you can say what you like, but I'm perfectly certain that you should have earthed them over. I mean to say in a climate like this with late frosts and God knows what . . . I mean my point is this, that it stands to reason. . . .

PROUT. Reason's got nothing to do with it. It's a matter

[18]

of experience. You only plant the roots. You leave the rest of the onion above ground.

MUTCH. Well, I'm perfectly certain that's wrong.

PROUT. My dear fellow, it's no use evolving methods of growing onions out of your inner consciousness. You can only grow imaginary onions that way. And what's the good of an imaginary onion ? It won't cheat you of a sigh or charm you to a tear.

MUTCH. But if a thing is logically and demonstrably wrong, surely to goodness. . . .

PROUT. You don't know what you're talking about.

MUTCH. Neither do you.

PROUT. That's perfectly true, but a jobbing gardener told me——

MUTCH. But nobody would be a jobbing gardener if he had any intellectual capacity whatever. I mean to say, it's notorious. . . .

PROUT. You'd better ask your wonderful Brains Trust if you want to know how to grow onions.

MUTCH. But we are the Brains Trust.

PROUT. Speak for yourself, I'm not going.

MUTCH. You damned well are.

PROUT. My dear Puggy. . . .

MUTCH. Now what in the world made you call me that ? Wasn't it funny ? I haven't been called Puggy for twenty-five years.

PROUT. I don't know. Funny that.

MUTCH. Anyhow you must admit there's something *wrong* with the onions.

PROUT. I know that ; but it's nothing to do with the way they were planted. You don't suppose I would plant onions without getting some sort of expert advice ? Good heavens ! I know my own limitations.

[RE-ENTER ANGELA.

MUTCH. Then what are you talking about ?

PROUT. Hullo.

[19]

ANGELA. Are you two quarrelling again?

PROUT. More or less, but you needn't look so pleased about it. We're not quarrelling about you.

ANGELA. Oh.

[ANGELA *starts to clear the tea-things on to the tray.*

ANGELA. That was quite interesting.

PROUT. What was?

ANGELA. That girl.

PROUT. What was interesting about her? A very ordinary type I thought.

ANGELA. It was her little romance that was interesting.

MUTCH. What? With the mechanic?

ANGELA. No. She's madly in love with the Padre.

PROUT. Don't be so damned silly. He's not that sort.

ANGELA. I didn't say he was in love with her, but she was watching him all the time out of the corners of her eyes. She was frightened to look at him for fear of giving herself away, except when our backs were turned. And she keyed herself up whenever he opened his mouth. Besides, what do you think she was talking about?

MUTCH. She was talking about education. She seemed to have some sort of mystical regard for it.

ANGELA. Mystical all right!

[*She picks up the tray.*

Mind you I don't think he has the least idea that she's crazy about him.

PROUT. You think everybody's crazy about somebody else. You should write musical comedies.

MUTCH. Let me help you with that tray.

ANGELA. Oh, don't bother, Jimmy.

MUTCH. I insist.

ANGELA. You're a perfect gentleman.

[*Gives him the tray.*

PROUT. Not like me I suppose.

ANGELA. Not a bit like you.

[MUTCH *goes out with the tray.*

PROUT. I suppose that unfortunate love-lorn stiff will wash the dishes.

ANGELA. Don't be so vulgar.

PROUT. I thought we were supposed to be.

ANGELA. What do you mean by that?

PROUT. Well, you've just been poking your nose into the amours of a little A.T. driver who's got nothing to do with you.

ANGELA. Everybody has to do with everybody else. We can't all lead utterly selfish lives like you.

PROUT. I'm selfish, am I?

ANGELA. Yes, very.

[RE-ENTER MUTCH.

PROUT. Aren't you going to wash up?

MUTCH. Oh, do you want me to?

PROUT. Of course. It isn't my turn.

ANGELA. Let them alone. I'll give them a wallop round when we're getting the supper ready. Sit down, you must be tired.

[MUTCH *throws himself down on the settee.*

MUTCH. Do you know, I think you're right.

ANGELA. Right about what, Jimmy?

MUTCH. About the A.T. She had that sort of faithful dog look.

PROUT. You don't call female dogs, dogs.

ANGELA. He can if he likes—go on, Jimmy. Besides, she isn't.

MUTCH. Of course not. She looks a very decent little girl to me. What does she see in him, do you think? And she's engaged to another fellow.

ANGELA. I expect she thinks he's a perfect gent. She's quite right, so he is.

MUTCH. She raised two very interesting points.

ANGELA. Yes, she did. What were they by the way—I forget.

MUTCH. Well, there was a point about whether one should marry into a higher intellectual level than one's own with the idea of making some sort of positive profit. There ought to be some sort of biological gain in that, if you see what I mean. I mean if they have offspring.

ANGELA. Yes, but it cuts both ways, doesn't it? If one marries up the other marries down.

MUTCH. Yes, on the intellectual plane. But we've got to consider the physical plane too. What you lose on the shies you make up on the round-abouts.

ANGELA. I see. What was the other point?

MUTCH. Oh, whether an intellectual background fits one specially to solve the problems of life.

ANGELA. I should have thought there was no doubt about that.

MUTCH. I wonder.

PROUT. An intellectual background wasn't much help to you in attacking the problem of spring onions. I'm going out to have a look at them. I'll try instinct and experience.

MUTCH. Instinct's got nothing to do with it, and you've had no experience.

PROUT. No, but the gardener has.

[EXIT PROUT. *Short silence.*

ANGELA. No, but honestly. . . .

MUTCH. Honestly what?

ANGELA. It is rather touching, isn't it?

MUTCH. You mean the little atsie?

ANGELA. Yes.

MUTCH. An infant crying in the night, an infant crying for the light, and with no language save a cry.

ANGELA. Yes. I wish we could help her. We ought to be able to help her.

MUTCH. What exactly do you mean by " help her "?

ANGELA. You of all people ought to know.

MUTCH. Well, I don't quite know what line you think we ought to take. Should we do a bit of fifth column work on the Padre, I mean to say? And then help her to break down his defences? I mean to say she'd probably be much better off with Walter.

ANGELA. No, no, no, no, no. I don't mean that at all. No. I mean, these people haven't been taught to think clearly and straightly and *starkly*. When they get into an emotional tangle they don't know what to do. I found that out when Polly Wotherspoon used to take me down to her Girls' Club. I mean they simply didn't know what I was talking about; and I'm a simple enough soul.

MUTCH. Yes, you are.

ANGELA. But what about this girl?

MUTCH. What about her?

ANGELA. Well, you know as well as I do that these unsolved problems grow into complexes and complexes grow into neuroses. Now I should think this girl has a very good brain. Not a first-class brain, and undeveloped, of course. But I think one could make something of her.

MUTCH. The difficulty is to make some sort of contact. I mean to say, after all, in the name of goodness, she doesn't speak our language.

ANGELA. Yes. Yes. There's that.

MUTCH. And should anyone, I mean, interfere in anyone else's life? I mean to say it never comes off.

ANGELA. But, Jimmy. It isn't interfering if somebody who can't swim falls into the water and you've had swimming lessons and dive in after them.

MUTCH. Yes. There's that. But I've a feeling it's a false analogy.

ANGELA. Not at all. She's floundering and splashing and puffing and blowing. She doesn't know what to do. It's a perfect analogy.

MUTCH. Well, you may be right.

ANGELA. And she wants our help. She promised to come to tea.

MUTCH. She said she'd ask the Brains Trust too.

ANGELA. Yes, she did. But I don't see much good in that. You can't answer questions like that in a Brains Trust.

MUTCH. Why not ? I mean to say, what's the use of sitting there and answering questions that don't matter ?

ANGELA. I wonder what her question's going to be. I wonder whether we can answer it.

MUTCH. Oh well, after all, I mean to say, one has a good deal of experience in answering much more complicated questions than this girl is likely to excogitate.

ANGELA. Yes—you are clever, Jimmy.

MUTCH. Oh, good heavens. I mean to say, it's my job, that kind of cleverness.

ANGELA. All the same, if you don't mind my saying so, do you know I sometimes think you—intellectualise—*things*—a little too much ?

MUTCH. Well, now, perhaps it is quite true that I have a sort of a tendency to sublimate emotions and impulses into some sort of rationalised and connected intellectual system. But why not ? I mean to say, we have developed ratiocinating faculties no doubt for some sort of coherent purpose—or at least as part of a more or less intelligible process. And after all there's a certain satisfaction in the exercise of one's more highly developed faculties.

ANGELA. Yes . . . I suppose so . . . yes. I suppose there *is* a certain satisfaction.

MUTCH. Well, I mean, isn't there ? I mean, take you and me. I mean, there you are.

ANGELA. Yes.

[*They look at one another. It almost seems as if they were about to exercise their less highly developed faculties when* PROUT *shouts.*

PROUT (*calling without*). Jimmy !
MUTCH. Yes, George ?

[HE *gets up.*

What is it ?

[24]

PROUT. Come here a minute—I want you.
MUTCH. Right-ho.

[EXIT MUTCH.

[ANGELA *blows her nose rather loudly and* EXITS *by the
curtained doorway.*

CURTAIN

END OF ACT I

ACT II

[*The scene is the stage of a Recreation Hut in some
military centre or other in Scotland. It is set for the
first scene of an old-fashioned pantomime. The village
inn is on one side and the squire's manor is on the
other. The scenery is extremely shabby. A long deal
table is set downstage with seven Windsor chairs
behind it. The lighting is very brilliant.*

[*The* PADRE *in battle dress and clerical collar bustles in.
He notices that the curtain is up and turns to
the audience after laying a sheaf of papers on the
table.*

PADRE. I say, excuse me, won't you? We've got the curtain up rather prematurely. Oh dear, what a frightful glare of lights; I must do something about it. Jessie! I won't be a minute. . . . Electrics! Jessie!

[ENTER JESSIE *in khaki dungarees.*

Look here, Jessie, we can't sit here below all these lights. We'd be blinded. Look, could you take down those thingumi- bobs a bit and put on the amber floats? You see what I mean? We don't want to be blinded.

JESSIE. Rightio.

[EXIT JESSIE *to Prompt side.*

[*The lights begin to go through a series of vagaries.*

[*Green light.*

PADRE. Oh, no, not green, Jessie, anything but green.

[*Amber foots alone.*

PADRE. Yes, that's all right, but look, Jessie, it's here we want the light, here on the table.

[*Foots off—white glare at the back. Doesn't see them for
a moment then looks.*

[26]

PADRE. No, no, Jessie, we're sitting down there.

> [*Lights change to moderate lighting.*

PADRE. Look now, Jessie, can you hear me? I only wanted the slightest modification.

> [*Black out.*
>
> [*Discovers audience.*

PADRE. Jessie, now please keep your head, and bring up your ambers ; Jessie, you must have ambers.

> [*Ambers up and foots.*

PADRE. Now we're getting somewhere, Jessie—now just a little bit more on the table.

> [*Foots out.*

Jessie, I said leave it at that.

> [*Lights properly.*
>
> [*The stage is gradually lit by an unconventional but rather agreeable glow.*

PADRE. I'm terribly sorry, ladies and gentlemen. Walter, the electrician has had a motor bicycle accident and I'm afraid Jessie isn't quite up to it yet. He recommended her, but, you see, she's his fiancée and perhaps his judgment was a little bit biassed. I don't know whether she's responsible for the rather *exotic* setting. Most of you saw the A.T.S. pantomime last night. I confess I feel a bit like a demon king.

> [*Black out. Red light.*
>
> [EXIT PADRE.

Ad lib   [JESSIE ENTERS, *sits down in front of Proscenium and begins to eat an apple.* RE-ENTER PADRE *ushering in the* BRAINS TRUST :—LADY DODD, ANGELA, MUTCH, JOE BYRES, DR. MACADAM *and* GEORGE PROUT. *They sit down at the table in the following order :—* BYRES, PROUT, LADY DODD, PADRE, MRS. PROUT, MUTCH, MACADAM. *The* PADRE *at once rises.*

PADRE. Ladies and gentlemen, it is my pleasant duty as Question Master to introduce to you tonight's Brains Trust.

On my extreme right, without further ado, is Mr. George Prout. He is a very celebrated painter of—er—oil paintings. He is a—a—Member of the Royal Institute of—of—Oil Painters. A very distinguished body of men who—who paint oil paintings. If there are any questions about art, I feel perfectly certain he will be able to deal with them—especially if they have anything to do with—ah—oil paintings. Next to him, I am very happy to be able to tell you, is Professor James Alexander Mutch, of the University of Skerryvore, and, at one time, of Balliol College, Oxford. He is a great expert on Metaphysics—and has written several books on the subject—besides being a well known anthropologist and one of our best known collectors of postage stamps. So if there are any questions about metaphysics or postage stamps, I am sure that they will be very ably dealt with——Jessie, must you sit there ? Can't you get a seat ?

JESSIE. I'm sorry, sir, I can't hear from the switchboard. I won't get in your way.

PADRE. But are you comfortable ?

JESSIE. Oh, quite, thank you.

PADRE. I need not introduce Lady Dodd. Many of us have been, I hope, welcome visitors to her house and grounds and to her kennels and we are under a very deep debt of gratitude to her. Lady Dodd is, as you know, the President of the County Branch of the Friends of the Fourfooted, Feathered and Furry. This by no means exhausts her activities, but perhaps I can spare her blushes and pass on to Mrs. Prout—I hardly know whether to call her Mrs. Prout or Angela Kilpatrick. She is the author of several delightful books—often of poetry—and has edited a children's magazine. She also is very interested in puppets and will, perhaps, some day, give us a little show. Will you ? Thank you so much. Then we have our old friend Dr. Macadam—a distinguished graduate in medicine of, I believe, Edinburgh University. Then we are very happy to have with us Mr. Joe Byres, who is a Member of Parliament for the Borough of Baikie. We have no politics here and we are very happy to have him with us. And now we shall get down to the business of the evening. The questions are on anything that comes up your backs. The Brains Trust hasn't seen any of them. I've picked them more or less as they come. Naturally I have barred questions on politics and religion and questions showing ill-timed facetiousness. We really can't discuss politics or religion in a mixed gathering like this and, of course the C.O. won't have smut. What's left makes a pretty good lot.

The first is from Leading Aircraftswoman Dixon. She asks, "What makes cows in a field run after railway trains?" Perhaps we might ask Lady Dodd to kick off. Now, Lady Dodd, "What makes cows in a field run after railway trains?" (*Sits.*)

LADY DODD. Well, now. That *is* a question! I've often wondered myself. My aunt was a great friend of Sir James Barrie and he told her that they were running to catch any babies that might fall out of the windows. I hardly think it can be that, though, mind you, cows are frightfully intelligent. They have such speaking eyes. I often wonder what they are speaking about. If we only knew!

PADRE. Thank you, Lady Dodd. Professor?

MUTCH. Well, I mean to say, are we entitled to suppose that they have any, at least, I mean, reason in point of fact for running after the train at all, if you follow me?

LADY DODD. Oh, they must have, they must have!

MUTCH. Well, I don't know. When one talks about *reason*, I mean to say one is going head over heels into the psychological aspect, and, I mean, after all, *have* cows a psychological aspect? I mean to say, we don't know enough about it. It may be a simple problem in bio-physics. But we simply don't know. Do we? I mean, you see my point?

PADRE. Yes, of course. Thank you. Mr. Byres?

BYRES. They get excited by the noise and the clatter. You'll no' see cows running in a field where a lot of trains pass.. They get used to it.

PADRE. Thank you. Mrs. Prout?

ANGELA. I agree with Mr. Byres. I think any kind of vague tumult is exciting and makes us want to jump or run or something. I think they run after the train instead of away from it because they like it. They like the monotony to be broken. Cows have very monotonous lives, you must remember.

PROUT. I don't agree. Most human beings live far more monotonous lives than cows. And if there's one thing they hate it's to have the monotony broken. Besides, cows don't run after trains.

ANGELA. Yes, they do, George.

PROUT. No, they don't. Anyhow, cows are females. What's the good of worrying about why they do anything on the living earth?

PADRE. Order, order! Dr. Macadam. Perhaps you will sum up.

MACADAM. What? What was the question?

PADRE. Why do cows run after railway trains?

MACADAM. I haven't the slightest idea.

PADRE. Well, I think we've had very varied and satisfactory answers to that most interesting question. I think the Trust has decided that it would be unwise to go too far into the cow's motives. . . . The next question is a very interesting one. It is from 857643 Lance Corporal Jenks W., of the Corps of Military Police. Corporal Jenks asks: "What are the guiding principles that lead a community to accept a canon of aesthetic values?" Yes. . . .

LADY DODD. What on earth does that mean?

PADRE. Now you're asking me! I think it means, if you look at a picture, say, or a lot of chaps look at a picture and say, "By Jove, that's jolly good," what makes them think so? I think this is Mr. Prout's cup of tea. Come along now, Mr. Prout, you're an artist. (*Sits.*)

PROUT. The only man who knows how to look at pictures is the man who paints them.

PADRE. Oh, come, come, come, !

ANGELA. What nonsense, George!

LADY DODD. I don't think myself. . . .

[30]

PROUT. There are plenty of idiots who chatter about pictures, but for all they see they might have one glass eye and the other stuffed with treacle. It makes me sick.

BYRES. You might as well say the only one who appreciates you is your mother.

PROUT. That's quite true. She *is* the only one. Was, rather, she's dead.

LADY DODD. I'm so sorry.

PROUT. Not at all.

PADRE. Perhaps we should pass on to the next question. Gunner McGuire wants to know if civilisation is, in the opinion of the Brains Trust, a failure; and what is civilisation anyway? We ought to have some good answers to that. Mrs. Prout?

ANGELA. We had better answer the second part first, hadn't we?

PADRE. As you wish. " What is civilisation, anyway? "

ANGELA. Civilisation, surely, is the application of knowledge and experience to the good of the greatest number of people.

PROUT. Oh, is it? You count a certain number of fat heads, and then try how far whatever you've got'll go round? That's not civilisation. You can have a civilisation if you've got half a dozen sensible men and a thousand million mugs. But the mugs have no part in it.

BYRES. They haven't, haven't they? Then it's high time they had.

PADRE. Oh—ah—well, I'm afraid we're getting perilously near politics. Perhaps Lady Dodd can give us an idea of what she understands by " civilisation " and whether she thinks it's a failure.

LADY DODD. Oh, I don't think it's a failure at all. There are lots of things one would like to see altered—but I think that on the whole we can say that we are making for righteousness. And nobody could say during this war, at any rate, that we are not a united nation moving forward in a common cause.

[31]

PADRE. I think we are all very much indebted to Lady Dodd for her very frank and penetrating answer.

MUTCH (*Hand up*).

PADRE. Oh, you wish to say something, Professor?

MUTCH. Well, I suppose I ought to say something, as it's a matter I've thought about a good deal. I mean to say, we must start, I mean, *this is important*. . . . We must start by having absolutely clear ideas about what we mean by what we are talking about. . . . I mean to say, it isn't as if there had only been one civilisation. There have been dozens and dozens and dozens. It's hopeless . . . . I mean, you've got to get down to brass tacks. I could go on all night about that, but perhaps I'd better not.

PADRE. Perhaps not. Thank you very much. Mr. Byres? (*Shaking his finger playfully.*) But no politics mind. What do you think of civilisation?

BYRES. I don't think much of it.

PADRE. Well, that's very much to the point. Well, I think I may say that the Brains Trust thinks that there is a great deal to be said for civilisation as we know it, and that there is life in the old dog yet.

BYRES. At the same time I must say that a civilisation built from top to bottom out of humbug, class-privilege and the profit motive is about as fancy a bit of jerry-building as ever I heard of. You'll see the whole jinghang come down with a fine-like clatter.

PADRE. Quite, Mr. Byres. Now we'll get along to the next question.

PROUT. But I agree with every word you say. Every beautiful device that we human beings have invented to keep the gorillas and yahoos in order will be destroyed.

BYRES. What do you mean by gorillas and yah-hoos?

PROUT. I mean your sacred proletariat.

BYRES. Well, I'm blessed! Who do you think you are, anyhow? The Chairman here says you make your living by painting pictures. I haven't seen any of your pictures, but what are pictures anyway? A bit of bourgeois decoration.

My wee girl of twelve paints pictures. But if I catch her putting on airs because she can put down on paper a thing that looks like a horse or a chrysanthemum, she'd get the skelping of her life.

PADRE. Order, order! We must get on to the next question

PROUT. Tickle my catastrophe! You can't argue with anybody. You can only bluster and rant. I never met a Labour politician who could do anything but bluster and rant.

BYRES. Oh, is that so? Well, if you're asking for home truths you'll get them; and if you're asking for a punch on the nose, you'll get it.

PADRE. Order! Order! Really, Mr. Byres. Really, Mr. Prout. I think you're both out of order, if you don't mind my saying so.

BYRES. Well, I demand an apology.

PROUT. Well then, I apologise.

BYRES. I accept your apology.

PADRE. Well, that's very nice. Very nice, indeed. And now we'll get along to the next question. It is a most interesting question sent in from Bombardier Benskin. Bombardier Benskin wants to know whether there is any evidence for the belief that living creatures exist on the moon's surface?

MUTCH. On the what?

PADRE. On the surface of the moon. Well, Professor? Perhaps we'll ask you to answer this question. Is there any evidence of life on the surface of the moon?

MUTCH. No.

PADRE. I beg your pardon?

MUTCH. No.

PADRE. Oh . . . We . . . You mean there's no evidence whatever?

MUTCH. No.

LADY DODD. None at all?

MUTCH. No.

LADY DODD. That seems very peculiar to me.

[33]

PADRE. Well, I think we must take it, Bombardier Benskin, there's no evidence of life on the moon. We come now to the next question. The next question is from Quartermaster Sergeant Murdo MacPherson. It reads as follows : " What is planning ? Who does it ? And who is going to carry out the plans ? " I think we ought to ask the Professor what he understands by planning ?

MUTCH. Well, it depends what you mean by planning.

PROUT. We're asking what *you* mean by planning ?

MUTCH. Well, I mean, to say, isn't planning a sort of synthesis of correlated probabilities interdigitated into a sort of a—kind of a—well, *pattern*—with the ultimate idea of translating the resulting probabilities into some—some sort of concrete matrix ? I should think that's perfectly clear.

PADRE. Well. . . .

ANGELA. But who is to *do* this planning ? Experts ? Or just anybody ?

MUTCH. Oh, experts, of course.

PROUT. Experts at what ?

MUTCH. Experts on planning.

LADY DODD. But who are these experts ? I wouldn't go so far as to say the Labour Party is unfit to govern—I knew Ramsay MacDonald very well—a charming man ; and my husband was at school with Mr. Attlee. But, there it is. Organising a whole huge Empire isn't a very easy matter. I think the people who run the show ought to have some experience and *background*. Or don't you think so, Professor ?

MUTCH. Oh yes, certainly. I think that's an absolute necessity. I mean to say, but of course, it depends on what background exactly. That is most important. I mean to say it's quite hopeless if you don't . . . well, take, for example——

PROUT. What it boils down to is, who is going to be boss ? And you and I will have damned little to say to that.

LADY DODD. You're what used to be called a mugwump, aren't you, Mr. Prout ?

PROUT. I am, and proud of it.

[34]

ANGELA. Well, you shouldn't be. I think this Brains Trust could run the Empire very well.

JESSIE. I don't.

PADRE. I beg your pardon?

JESSIE. Nothing. Sorry.

ANGELA. Wait a minute. Why don't you think so?

JESSIE. If you're going to order a lot of human beings about you've got to be human, see? This Brains Trust isn't human.

PADRE. Allowing for the fact that the interruption is entirely out of order, Jessie, and if I may be permitted to make a mild observation, I should say that if this Brains Trust has a fault it is that it has been a little too human so far.

JESSIE. It can't be too human, but you're all ladyships and M.P.s and artists and things. Look at the professor. He's not human.

MUTCH. You're a damned liar.

PADRE. Oh, I say, come, come, order, order.

JESSIE. Well show it then. You've been asked all sorts of questions what human beings are ever so interested in and all you do is show off, and not very well either at that.

PADRE. Really, Jessie, I can't allow this sort of thing.

ANGELA. But I want to know what this girl's driving at. If my husband and I aren't human I don't know who is.

JESSIE. Perhaps you are in your way. Okey-doke, carry on.

PADRE. With the young lady's kind permission we will carry on. The next question is from—let me see—Private— oh, dear me—something—it looks like Hezekiah. No. It's . . . Private J.B. I can't make this out.

JESSIE. Killigrew.

PADRE. Eh? What?

JESSIE. Killigrew, Jessie Killigrew.

PADRE. Oh, it's you, Jessie?

JESSIE. Yes, it's me.

PADRE. That's very interesting. Jessie wants to know whether . . . I can't make it out. It looks like marshmallow.

[35]

JESSIE. Is marriage a good idea ?

PADRE. I beg your pardon ? I wish you wouldn't speak with your mouth full.

JESSIE. That's the question. Is marriage a good idea ? And if it is what's the best way to choose a partner ?

PADRE. I thought it was marshmallow. Very stupid of me. Well then, Private Jessie Killigrew would like to know whether, in the opinion of the Brains Trust, marriage is a good idea. Lady Dodd ?

LADY DODD. I think it's an excellent idea. I think that, perhaps, with the exception of kindness to animals, it is one of the best ideas in the world ; except Christianity, of course. But Christianity takes it all in, doesn't it ? I mean they wouldn't let us get married in churches unless it were a frightfully good plan, would they ? Anyhow, I'm married, and very glad I am, although poor Lord Dodd is a martyr to osteo-arthritis as many of you know.

PADRE. Thank you, Lady Dodd. Dr. Macadam, you have been very silent. What do you think about it ?

MACADAM. I am sorry. I didn't catch the question.

PADRE. Is marriage a good idea ?

MACADAM. I don't know whether it's a good idea or a bad idea, but it's an inevitable idea. Mind you, it's a contract very few sane people would enter into ; but, in point of fact, hardly any sane people do enter into it.

LADY DODD. Oh, Doctor, what a dreadful thing to say !

MACADAM. What was that ?

LADY DODD. I said that was an awful thing to say.

MACADAM. Well, it's quite true. If falling in love isn't going mad, I've never seen a lunatic. It's a state of sub-acute mania with alternations of exaltation and depression and persistent hallucinations. Nobody's fit to make a contract in such a state.

LADY DODD. Then how—oh, I beg your pardon (*to Padre*)— do you account for the fact that there are thousands and thousands of happy marriages ? People do live happy ever after.

MACADAM. Happy ever after ? Of course they are, some of them. Anyone can get on with anybody else if he tries hard enough. If I went blindfolded to any cinema queue and picked out a female, she and I could live happily enough ever after if we had to. And that's how it's done, I solemnly assure you.

BYRES. If it's as easy as all that, why didn't you get married ?

MACADAM. Because I never went mad. We'd have no marriages unless we went mad, and we'd be in a fine mess without it.

PADRE. Oh, thank you, Doctor. Well, now, Mrs. Prout ?

ANGELA (*gently*). I must have been mad when I got married.

PROUT. That's a nice thing to say in public.

JESSIE. Never mind about the public. Get on with it.

PADRE. Really, Jessie ! This is getting to be a bit too much of a good thing.

JESSIE. But I want to know. Me and my boy-friend has had words about it, and the pictures are all hooey, and the books are just daft. If you ladies and gents, with all this background that we hear so much about, can't settle a thing like that I don't think much of you. Only you've got to be human— honest you have.

[PADRE *attempts to interrupt.*

ANGELA. It's all right. I'll do my best. I remember when I first met George. The only thing I thought about him was that I didn't think his finger nails were very clean, and he hadn't shaved properly. There was a horrid little bit of stubble at the angle of his jaw.

JESSIE. That's a bit more like it.

PROUT. To be perfectly candid I didn't think you were much to look at either. You had a way of flinching whenever you said anything ; it irritated me abominably.

ANGELA. I remember noticing a rather peculiar and distinctly unpleasant smell. It is rather difficult to describe.

PADRE. I don't think you need attempt to describe it here, Mrs. Prout.

[37]

ANGELA. Well, it wasn't a religious smell and it wasn't a political smell. There was some turpentine and some rather stale tobacco. (PROUT *turns away*.) Perhaps that's why I flinched. I was out for a walk with my puppy I remember, and he suddenly began to bite Mr. Prout's shoes. That's how we got to know each other.

LADY DODD. The darling ! What kind of puppy was he ?

ANGELA. He was an Aberdeen terrier.

LADY DODD. There's no love like a dog's love, is there ?

PROUT. He was a filthy little brute called Sambo. He bit through my last shoe-lace. I didn't like him any better at first sight than I liked his mistress. She looked like a bit of damp sea-weed ; she had a cold in the head.

ANGELA. It wasn't a very bad cold. It was just starting.

PROUT. It was quite bad enough.

ANGELA. Perhaps it's true to say that I wasn't looking my best.

PROUT. But your best isn't much either. . . . What the devil did we talk about ? I forget.

ANGELA. Wait a bit. I was just coming out of our house on the main street. My father was a country solicitor, you know. We had an old house right on the High Street with a most beautiful walled garden at the back with a little green gate and steps running down to the river.

[*Goes up steps.* JESSIE *rises.*

Do you remember, George ?

PROUT. Yes, I remember.

[ANGELA *wanders about up-stage in a vague manner.*

ANGELA. On the day we are speaking about I was going out to buy butter, and I thought I'd just take Sambo for very nearly his first walk. George was just coming out of the pub.

JESSIE. Like that pub over there ?

ANGELA. Yes. It was called the " Fox and Grapes." It was very like that pub.

PROUT (*jumping up*). Yes, by Jove. I remember thinking it

[38]

it was like a scene in a pantomime. The village street, I mean.
The village green was up there, nearly as green as that. The
main street ran down right where you chaps are sitting.   The
pub and the lawyer's house were just at the top of it. I was
living in the pub.

JESSIE (*excitedly*). Go into it. It's only a canvas pub. But
go into it now. We'll reconstruct the crime like they do in the
" Who Done Its."

PROUT. Shall we ? All right.

JESSIE. Hurry up, get cracking. Double march.

[PROUT *responds to the command and trots into the pub.*

ANGELA. Shall I go into the Manor ?

JESSIE. Yes, yes. Go on.

ANGELA. I had a cold. I always had a cold in the early
spring.

[SHE *disappears through the doorway of the Manor.*

JESSIE (*shouting*). A February morning, Mrs. Prout ?

ANGELA (*off*). Yes. 18th of February.

JESSIE. Right-ho. I'll fix it.

PADRE. Dear me, isn't this a little unusual ? I don't know
whether——Jessie !

BYRES. Let's have the next question.

PADRE. Do you think so ? Well, now, let me see——

[*Black out. Then raw lighting with plenty of blue in it.*

Good gracious me, what's happening to the lights ?
Jessie must be doing something to them.

[RE-ENTER JESSIE, *buttoning on her A.T.S. uniform
jacket. She is wearing a hat.*

What on earth have you done to the lights ?

JESSIE. Sorry, sir—trying to make a February morning.

PADRE. Why on earth do you want to make a February
morning ?

JESSIE. Mrs. Prout wanted one.

PADRE. Well, really, this is supposed to be a Brains Trust.

How can the Trust use its brains if this sort of thing keeps on happening ?

JESSIE.   I'll give you a hand if you like, sir.

PADRE.   What do you mean you'll give us a hand ?

JESSIE.   They teach us in the A.T.S. to use our brains in time of emergency.   May I sit down, sir ?

PADRE.   Well, you seem to be running the whole show anyhow.   I don't see why you shouldn't.

JESSIE.   Thank you, sir.

BYRES.   Come and sit beside me, Jessie.

[JESSIE *sits in* PROUT'S *seat.*

PADRE.   Now may we go on ?

JESSIE.   Sorry !   Certainly.

PADRE.   And now, perhaps, we can consider——Good heavens, what's the matter, Mrs. Prout ?

[ENTER ANGELA *from the Manor House.   She goes through the motions of leading an imaginary dog.*

JESSIE.   Sh . . . . please, sir.

ANGELA.   Now Sambo, be a good doggie and go right inside.   Cook's got a nice bone for you if you behave like a good, decent little doggie.   You can't come for a walk with Angy.   Do you hear me ?   You can't.   Come here at once you bad dog.

[PROUT ENTERS *from the inn carrying an imaginary easel and painting materials.   He stumbles over the imaginary dog.*

PROUT.   Ough !   Get out of the way, you little brute.   You nearly had me down.

ANGELA.   I'm so sorry.   He's only a baby.

PROUT.   Oh, that's all right.

ANGELA.   Come here at once, you bad dog.   You are very naughty and disobedient.

PROUT.   Run along—do what you're told.   You mustn't eat my feet.   They're not nourishing.

ANGELA. Sambo!

> [SHE *runs forward and gathers the imaginary dog into her arms.*

No licks now, you bad, bad dog. Angy's not friends with you any more. What a whipping you're going to get.

PROUT. I shouldn't beat him if I were you. You'll spoil his temper.

ANGELA. Hush! I've no intention of giving him a B-E-A-T-I-N-G; but he understands every word we say.

PROUT. Oh, come, come.

ANGELA. Yes, he does. These little Scotties are terribly intelligent.

PROUT. They've their own kind of intelligence, of course, but how can they understand spoken language?

ANGELA. I don't know. . . . I don't see how anybody can know. . . . Oh, look, he's bitten through your shoe-lace.

PROUT. So he has, damn him.

ANGELA. Do just wait a minute, I'll get another for you. There are some lying on the hall table. I bought them from a hawker this morning.

PROUT. Oh, not at all. Please don't trouble. I can tie the ends together.

ANGELA. No, no, it's no trouble at all.

> [SHE *runs into the house.* PROUT *sits down on the step and begins to work with his shoelace.* ANGELA *appears almost immediately with a new lace.*

ANGELA. Take your shoe off and I'll lace it up for you. There's nobody about; or would you—would you care to come in?

PROUT. Oh, no thanks, it's quite all right, but do let me do it myself.

ANGELA. Not at all. It was my dog that did the damage.

> [SHE *laces the shoe.*

You should have come in; but to tell you the truth, I was ashamed to ask you in. Father's gone away for a

[41]

week's fishing and Cook and I are doing the spring cleaning.
And we're rather picnicking.

PROUT. You've no mother?

ANGELA. No, she died last year. Are you staying at the Inn?

PROUT. Yes, I've been staying there for a week. I'm going
tomorrow.

ANGELA. It isn't very comfortable at the Inn.

PROUT. No.

ANGELA. Do they give you enough to eat?

PROUT. Quite enough. More than enough. The trouble is
that it's uneatable.

ANGELA. Oh, I am sorry. I say, do come in for five minutes.
At least we've got a good fire and I'll get Cook to make you
a cup of tea.

PROUT. That is very tempting. (ANGELA *hands back shoe.*)
Oh, thank you. (*Takes shoe.*)

ANGELA. But I forgot. You want to go and paint.

PROUT. There's a flurry of sleet coming on. I don't think
I'll paint today.

[HE *puts on his boot.*

ANGELA. And one of your feet must be frozen. Yes, it is!
What a pig I am. Do come in and get warm. I'll keep the
puppy dog locked up.

PROUT. Well, it's most awfully kind of you. Thanks, I will.

[ANGELA *and* PROUT *go into the Manor.*

JESSIE (*getting up*). Excuse me a minute.

PADRE. What's the matter now?

JESSIE. I nearly forgot something.

PADRE. Forgot what?

JESSIE. The moon.

PADRE. She did say the moon? . . . .

[EXIT JESSIE.

Do you know I think that girl Jessie ought to see a
psychiatrist; I'll certainly see about that tomorrow. She
must see a psychiatrist.

[*Sudden dim to night and moon.*

[42]

Oh, my goodness. This is really too much. What's happening now ?

> [*The moon rises. Lights appear in the windows of the Manor and the pub. A fiddle is heard playing a rustic air.* ENTER ANGELA *and* PROUT *from the Manor House* RE-ENTER JESSIE. *She sits down again.*

JESSIE. Sorrow.

PROUT. How sweet the moonlight sleeps upon this bank.

ANGELA. The bank was at the other end of the street. It never seemed to be open.

PROUT. Strange things, banks. I want to take my boots off when I go into them, as if they were mosques.

ANGELA. Oh, I'm quite happy in banks. Father always banked at the next town. They talk so much in little villages. He never would have a telephone either. Father liked. . . . I mean he likes having secrets. I like them too. That's why I'll never be a real artist, like you.

PROUT. I'm a rotten artist.

ANGELA. Are you ? That's funny, I don't seem to care. And you have never asked me to read you one of my poems.

PROUT. I dare not.

ANGELA. You're afraid they wouldn't be good ?

PROUT. They might not be, and I might have to lie to you— or to myself. You are not the kind of person I want to tell lies to.

ANGELA. I feel exactly that about you too. It's very queer.

PROUT. You have one of those voices I find awfully attractive. Like a nightingale.

ANGELA. It's only a bad cold coming on. It isn't my usual voice.

PROUT. I say ! Ought you to be out ?

ANGELA. No, I don't think so. I ought to go in now.

PROUT. Have you any toddy in the house ?

ANGELA. No. Father's a very strict teetotaller.

PROUT. I'll fetch you a gill of whisky from the pub.

ANGELA. No, no. It's most frightfully kind of you, but you mustn't. I'll be all right.

PROUT. Are you sure?

ANGELA. Yes. It's nothing really. I throw them off very quickly. I'm never really ill.

PROUT. I can fetch it in a minute.

ANGELA. No, Mr. Prout. Positively no.

PROUT. Yes.

ANGELA. No, George, you mustn't. I'll say goodnight now.

PROUT. Tomorrow?

ANGELA. Yes.

PROUT. When?

ANGELA. Oh, any time. About ten.

PROUT. Nasty things, these colds. Hadn't you better stay in bed?

ANGELA. Oh, no. I'm not encouraged to go to bed when I have a cold. I've never learned the habit.

PROUT. Then I think it's a damned shame. You spend all your life thinking for others and working for others and you'll never get any thanks for it.

ANGELA. But I'm not that sort of person at all, Mr. Prout.

PROUT. I don't think you know what sort of person you are. Perhaps it's as well.

ANGELA. Why?

PROUT. Because that curious shy grace you've got might be lost. You're like a wild creature conscious of every leaf that stirs, but unconscious of yourself. I think it's the most important part of your charm. You see, you're not classically beautiful, though you've got interesting features and rather beautiful eyes. (*Takes her hand.*) And your hands are lovely. And there's a burnt amber note in your hair that reminds me of Manet. You don't walk very well, though you have a fascinating slouch—like a thoroughbred foal. I don't know what shape you are because of your hideous clothes; but the little sage-brush shadows round your mouth and at the angle of your jaw are a knock-out.

[44]

ANGELA. But you can't see me. It's too dark.

PROUT. I see you all the time. I can't get you out of my head. I never in my life met a human being who interested me so much. And yet I'm afraid of you.

ANGELA. Afraid of me? Why?

PROUT. I wish I knew. When a woman attracts me, I'm not usually afraid.

ANGELA. You are often attracted by women?

PROUT. My God, yes! But you're a different kettle of fish. I told you why.

ANGELA. Sh . . . . listen!

[*A clock chimes twelve.*

But that's dreadful. It's midnight. May I say something to you?

PROUT. Yes.

ANGELA. It's heavenly to have found a real friend at last. Goodnight.

PROUT. Goodnight, Angela.

ANGELA. Goodnight, George.

[*They embrace suddenly.* ANGELA *breaks away and runs into the house.* PROUT *stands gazing at the windows.* JESSIE *slips out and at once a light appears in a series of windows. After several trials she decides on one of them.*

PADRE. Well, now, thank you very much, Mr. Prout. Do sit down.

[*Stage is completely lit.* PROUT, *in some embarrassment, regains his seat.*

Well—er—yes. Er—I think we are all very much indebted to Mr. and Mrs. Prout for their demonstration and, no doubt, we all feel ourselves very much enlightened. But at the same time. . . .

[RE-ENTER JESSIE *with camp-stool. She sits at the* R. *end of the table.*

D   [45]

JESSIE. I think myself that's a silly scene.

PROUT. I know. So it is. That's the whole point of it.

[RE-ENTER ANGELA.

PADRE. Oh, there you are, Mrs. Prout. Thank you very much. Well, now, ladies and gentlemen——

ANGELA. Not at all.

[*She sits down.* JESSIE *is wandering about upstage.*

PADRE. Well . . . we've been getting, perhaps, a little astray. . . .

PROUT. Not at all. My wife and I behaved in that idiotic way because . . . because we were each carrying about with us a microscopic bit of matter that could neither read nor write, nor see, nor hear, nor speak, nor think. It had nothing but a will. But, somehow or other, that will could call to its neighbour and say, " Hullo. Let's get together and grow into a thing which is a perfectly arranged mixture of Angela and George—with her eyes and his nose— with her tendency to be chesty and his tendency to lose his temper." " Right," says the other gene, "The first thing to do is to make them both mad. He's a scruffy looking devil and with a face like a gargoyle. She's a long, lanky creature with knock-knees and a snivelling cold in the head. Let's make him think she's Venus and make her think he's Phoebus Apollo ; otherwise they'll never be such damned fools as to chain themselves together for the rest of their lives." The Doctor's quite right.

MACADAM. Eh ?

PROUT. I said you were quite right.

MACADAM. Right about what ? I didn't quite catch what you said. Would you mind repeating it ?

PROUT. What I said was . . . .

PADRE. Please, not again, Mr. Prout.

[*The* BRAINS TRUST *protests vigorously.*

JESSIE. But . . . oh, well.

PADRE. Jessie !

ANGELA. All the same, I don't think I was so frightful as all that.

PROUT. Yes, you were.

MUTCH. Nonsense.

PROUT. What's that?

MUTCH. Well, I mean to say, of course . . . .

JESSIE. Is that only what you think of her now, or did you think that then?

PADRE. I really, really must put a stop to this.

LADY DODD. Oh, but why? I think it's fascinating.

JESSIE. Don't you want us to learn something? I thought that's what Brains Trusts were for—to teach you something—and we've only just begun. We've seen that two people can get hooked up for life without knowing in the least what they're after.

LADY DODD. Oh, but it doesn't always happen that way. I think my husband knew what he was after when he married me.

[PADRE *sits with head in hands.*

JESSIE. But anyhow that's how it happened once. I want to know what comes next. Do they live happy ever after?

PROUT. Nobody lives happy ever after, but they get on all right.

ANGELA (*doubtfully*). Well. . . .

PROUT. What do you mean by " Well "? Oh, I know we have our ups and downs, and life would be pretty dull without an occasional row ; but personally I think we've made a darned good arrangement. We've had to give and take a bit, but that's a law of the Universe. I'm sometimes a bit unreasonable and Angela's never anything else, but it doesn't take long to find a *modus vivendi.*

JESSIE. A what?

PROUT. A way of living.

JESSIE. But is it the best way of living?

MUTCH (*thumping the table*). No, by God, it isn't.

[*A startled silence as they all look at* MUTCH.

MACADAM. What did you say ?   I didn't quite catch. . . .

MUTCH. I said it isn't. It's all right for George. He's got somebody to look after his laundry and cook his meals and fight with the tradesmen and listen to his ravings and tell him he's wonderful. But where in the name of all the suffering saints does Angela come in ? She's got a far better brain than he has. She's got all the qualities to make her name in the world, and she's got what he hasn't got—decent manners and the capacity for hard work. And she's got to stand like a conjuror's assistant flourishing a handkerchief and shouting "Voila" whenever he takes a mangy rabbit out of the hat. It makes me sick.

JESSIE. Yes, but how did it work out that way ?

MUTCH. I'll tell you. I'll tell you all right. It's just pure damned undiluted——

[MUTCH *rises in great excitement.*

PADRE. No. Stop. Sit down, please, Professor.

[MUTCH *sits down.* PADRE *looks at his wrist-watch.*

PADRE. Ladies and gentlemen, according to the programme we should have a little interval here, and I must say I think it is high time. Coffee and soft drinks will be served at the Canteen Bar for exactly ten minutes. After that I hope you will take your seats promtly for the second part of this Brains Trust session. May I say that I hope by that time certain of the distinguished members of the Trust will have composed themselves a little as we have several very interesting questions to discuss. Thank you very much. Ten minutes only.

[PADRE *bows to the* BRAINS TRUST, *who rise and file out, except* JESSIE, *who comes down into the audience.*

The CURTAIN *remains up.*

END OF ACT II

ACT III

Scene I

[*The* BRAINS TRUST *files in.*

[*The members of the* TRUST *let go a " feu de joie " of variegated coughs.* JESSIE *is not among them, but her camp-stool remains at the end of the table. The* PADRE *rises.*

PADRE. Well, now. We now begin the second part of this Brains Trust session, and you'll notice I've contrived somewhat less exotic surroundings. The first part was—I will not say marred—but a little disorganised by certain—shall I call them, eccentricities. But I think you'll find a cup of tea has put that all right, and I notice that Jessie has deserted us, so I think you will find that we are a little more—ah—usual in this part of the programme without, I hope, being in any way conventional. Now the first question is from Private Slater of the Royal Army Medical Corps. He wants to know what is meant by a sense of humour and how an effective sense of humour may be cultivated. Lady Dodd?

LADY DODD. Well, now, a sense of humour is a wonderful gift. I can't imagine what it must be like not to have one. I have a very keen sense of humour myself, and I have always been thankful for it. Deeply and truly thankful. As to cultivating a sense of humour, I think that can be done by subscribing to some such periodical as *Punch* and looking at the most amusing pictures. Then there are always books like Mark Twain's *Innocents Abroad*. My father used to read it aloud to us and we always laughed when he did, even if we didn't see the joke straight away.

PADRE. Thank you Lady Dodd. Dr. Macadam, I wonder if you heard the question.

MACADAM. Yes, yes, I'm not deaf.

PADRE. Have you any remarks to make then?

MACADAM. I haven't got a sense of humour myself. I'm too busy, but I notice some people are always giggling at something or other. People like that are usually a bit soft in the head. It's all damn nonsense.

BYRES. I don't know ; I think a good joke now and again keeps things going, so long as it's clean. Some things I hear on the B.B.C. I can hardly believe my ears ; but I'm partial to a good hearty laugh.

[*He relapses into a gloomy silence.* JESSIE ENTERS *from audience unobtrusively and takes her seat on the camp stool.*

PADRE. I'm sure you are, Mr. Byres (*Sees* JESSIE). Oh, you're back again.

JESSIE. Yes. Sorrow. I popped over to the hospital to see Walter.

PADRE. Oh, how is he ?

JESSIE. He's all right so far. I'm sorry I'm late. Go on.

PADRE. Well, I'm sure the Brains Trust is very grateful to you for your kind permission. We have just been discussing a sense of humour.

JESSIE. Oh, I'm sorry I missed that.

PADRE. Would you like to say anything about it ?

JESSIE. No. I want to hear more about Mr. and Mrs. Prout.

PADRE (*drops mallet*). My dear girl, you must try to control your curiosity. Mr. and Mrs. Prout are entitled to some measure of private life.

JESSIE. But I want to know about marriage.

PADRE. That was the last question but one.

JESSIE. But they haven't answered it yet.

PADRE. Oh, for heaven's sake. Well, Private Slater, the Brains Trust thinks that a sense of humour is difficult to define, but that it is a very valuable thing to have. We think you can cultivate one by reading suitable books and magazines, and refraining from listening to the B.B.C. We shall pass on to the next question. It is anonymous. The questioner wants to know how a bluebottle walking on the ceiling takes off when it wants to fly. A most interesting question. How does a bluebottle take off from the ceiling?

JESSIE. Who cares?

PADRE. Obviously the person who asked the question. Now Lady Dodd—you're a great animal lover. Do you know the explanation? How does a bluebottle take off from the ceiling?

LADY DODD. A bluebottle is not an animal.

JESSIE. That's right—it's an insect.

PADRE. Ah. Then perhaps Miss Killigrew, who seems to be so well informed in natural history, will enlighten us as to how a bluebottle takes off from the ceiling?

JESSIE. What a soppy question! It doesn't need to take off, at all. It just drops.

PADRE. That is your opinion?

JESSIE. That's right.

PADRE. Well, Doctor? How does a bluebottle take off from the ceiling?

MACADAM. Talking of a sense of humour. It's quite true that you do come across some laughable things in general practice. I remember an old fellow with a swelling on his backside the size of your head. . . .

PADRE. Yes, yes, Doctor, but. . . .

MACADAM. I had a surgeon in to see him, and we both agreed that we ought to take a wallop at it.

PADRE. Yes, but Doctor. . . .

MACADAM. So we just did the operation on the kitchen table with me giving the chloroform. I must say the young fellow made a good job of it.

PADRE. We're straying a little from the point.

MACADAM. As neat a bit of work as ever I saw. It left a beautiful scar. A credit to the surgeon.

PADRE. It's about bluebottles.

MACADAM. A pity the old fellow couldna show it—owing to its situation if you understand. But as I was saying.

PADRE. Yes, Doctor, but I'm afraid we're straying a little from the question. It's about bluebottles.

MACADAM. So we helped him into his concealed bed, and as soon as he came out of the chloroform he said. . . .

PADRE.   IT'S ABOUT BLUEBOTTLES ! BLUE-BOTTLES !

MACADAM. He didnae need a bottle, just a whiff. So this old fellow he felt under his pillow and took out a handful of dirty greasy notes and asked the doctor what his fee was. " Oh," says he, " ten guineas." So the old fellow went—one, two, three, four, five, six, seven, eight— and then says he, " You can take it or leave it. Eight pounds. And if you dinnae like it you can put the swallin' back."

PADRE. Yes, ha, ha. Quaint old characters you meet some-times. Well, the opinion of the Brains Trust about bluebottles is——

MACADAM. I mind another time when I was walking the hospital. . . .

PADRE. Yes, yes, quite, another time.

MACADAM. Aye, another time, I was just a laddie though, mind you, you'd have thought I was Joseph Lister and Syden-ham rolled into one.

PADRE. Will you tell us about it later, we have to get on ?

MACADAM. Surely, surely. It's all the same to me.

ANGELA. Do you know, I wish someone would explain to me how bluebottles manage to walk on the ceiling at all.

PROUT. Don't be so damned stupid.

MUTCH. That'll do.

PROUT. What's that ?

MUTCH. I said that'll do.

PROUT. Well, upon my word, Mr. Mutch, I don't see why the devil I can't make a remark to my wife without you brawling and blustering in.

ANGELA. He wasn't brawling, George.

PROUT. Yes, he was.

PADRE. Mr. Prout, please, please, please. And Professor, please to you too.

JESSIE. What's the matter ?

PADRE. What's the matter with what ?

JESSIE. What's the matter between these three ?

PADRE. There's nothing the matter you silly girl. Sit down and keep quiet.

JESSIE. There is, there is. And I want my question decently answered. It's a matter of life and death to me, Padre. I've got to tell Walter tonight.

PADRE (*holds* JESSIE). Jessie, Jessie, Jessie. Control yourself. You're getting quite hysterical.

JESSIE. No, I'm not. We never had hysterics in my family. We had to work too blooming hard. But I want to know.

PADRE. You want to know what ?

JESSIE. I want to know what happened. Everybody here wants to know. Come on, Mrs. Prout, get on with it.

PADRE. I can't allow this. I simply can't allow this. . . . Jessie, go away, go away at once.

JESSIE. No, no, please, sir, no. Please, Mrs. Prout—it means a lot to me. It means a lot to Walter too. Please, Mrs. Prout.

ANGELA. I—I—I don't know. I don't think I. . . .

[ANGELA *burst into tears.* MUTCH *leaves his seat and goes to her.*

MUTCH. It's all right. Don't worry, don't cry, I'll take you away.

PROUT. Take your hands off her, will you ?   (*To the* PADRE.) Get out of the way.

PADRE (*vaults table*). Now, now, Mr. Prout. Behave yourself.

[*He twists* PROUT's *arm round behind his back and gently levers him into his seat.*

I ought to tell you that I've done a bit of scrapping in my time. I was amateur middle-weight champion of. . . .

PROUT. I know, I know. Like that damned swine Puggy there. Your sort of repartee is knocking people about like a couple of navvies. You'd dare to put your filthy paws on a man like me, you infernal bullies! Damned bullies, that's just what you are.

[HE *throws his head on his arms and begins to cry*

PADRE. Oh, dear me, what a state of affairs? What on earth am I to do? Jessie, let down the curtain.

JESSIE. No.

LADY DODD (*rising*). I think perhaps I'd better go.

PADRE. Jessie—let down that curtain. That's an order.

JESSIE. It's not working, sir.

PADRE. This is terrible. Mr. Prout. Pull yourself together, be a man and not a cry-baby. Lady Dodd, I'm most frightfully sorry—I don't know what to say.

LADY DODD. Oh, it isn't your fault. It's that girl's fault.

JESSIE. I didn't tell them to get married.

LADY DODD. I know that, but you bullied them into talking about it, with all these people looking on too. You ought to be ashamed of yourself.

JESSIE. Please, Lady Dodd, sit down for a minute please. Please, Professor, you too. Padre, please! Now I'll try to explain.

[*For want of anything better to do, they obey her.*

JESSIE. Listen. In our street in Civvy Street they never tell you about anything. They talk about things that have happened, but they never tell you how they happened, and it's all a mess. If you ask them they tell you nothing but lies. Them that have been through it, I mean. The young ones like ourselves, they'll talk about it, but what do they know? They don't know anything. And the pictures and the books are all lies too. I never see anyone that's got an education from one year's end to another, and now I've got you here you're going to stay here until you tell me whether it's worth while getting married or not. You said you were here to answer questions, so get on with them. Did you choose right or didn't you? And if you didn't, what was wrong?

[54]

Answer that one and you can bubble and scream as much as you like. I don't mind. We're used to it in our street.

[*Short silence.*

ANGELA (*drying her tears*). She's quite right, you know. We ought to answer her question.

PADRE. No, please ; I really must put my foot down. After all, I'm supposed to be the Question Master. Does the Brains Trust wish me to continue in that office, or would you rather I handed over to Private Killigrew ?

LADY DODD. No, no, please go on. You're doing splendidly.

BYRES. You're quite good enough.

PADRE. Well, if I am to be Question Master, I must insist on being Master ; I suppose, Mr. Byres would say that no man is good enough to be another man's master, but at the same time. . . . Jessie, do you want to be Question Mistress ?

JESSIE. No, I don't.

PROUT (*uncovering his face*). No woman is good enough to be another man's mistress.

PADRE. Order ! Order ! Now what do you want me to do ? Do you want me to go on to the next question or what ?

ANGELA. I still think we should answer Miss Killigrew's question.

PADRE. Lady Dodd.

LADY DODD. Oh, yes. But we needn't have any more of these horrid charades, need we ?

PADRE. I hope not. Mr. Byres ?

BYRES. Let the lassie have her way. We havnae answered her question yet.

PADRE. Professor ?

MUTCH. Oh, all right, all right.

PADRE. Mr. Prout ? Are you feeling better ? Would you care to continue this discussion ?

PROUT. *I* don't give a damn.

PADRE. Doctor ?

[55]

MACADAM. I didn't quite catch the question.

PADRE. Do you think we should go on discussing matrimony?

MACADAM. We've been discussing matrimony since the Garden of Eden. I don't see why we should stop now.

PADRE (*sighing*). Very well, then. Mrs. Prout, I think you had something to add.

ANGELA. Well, what exactly does Miss Killigrew want to know?

JESSIE. Oh, I know the facts of life, if that's what you mean. But I want to know how it works out.

ANGELA. I don't really know. You go mad more or less all of a sudden, but you recover quite slowly and by degrees. I suppose a family makes all the difference. We've had two— a boy and a girl. It was very exciting and very unpleasant. But perhaps Dr. Macadam could tell you more about that. He was our doctor both times, and the referee sees more of the game than the players.

PADRE. I hardly think we can ask Dr. Macadam to go into these—ah—obstetrical details.

JESSIE. Why did you stop having children?

ANGELA. It didn't seem a very good idea somehow. I mean they're all right in their way. They're charming kids.

JESSIE. What happened then?

PROUT. They grew up into a couple of devils incarnate. They made it impossible to work or think or do any mortal thing that wasn't centred on their caprices and inordinate desires.

ANGELA. They *were* hard to manage. We sent them away to school four years ago. The boy was eight and the girl was seven. Then we had time to notice each other again.

JESSIE. And what did you think of each other?

ANGELA. It's difficult to say. All these things happened so gradually. I think we felt very jolly and hearty and friendly and helpful, like people who have just been through a blitz. I mean to say, children get on your nerves deliberately, and most grown-ups try not to.

PROUT. They're not always very successful.

ANGELA. No, they're not always very successful. I began noticing things about George that I didn't like very much, and I suppose that hurt his vanity, because he began to lose his temper very often.

JESSIE. You stopped loving each other?

PROUT. What?

ANGELA. No, no, no. Of course not.

PROUT. Good heavens, no.

ANGELA. I wonder where you got that idea. It wasn't the same, of course, as it was at first; but you aren't the same as you were when you were three years old. George and I are devoted to each other.

PROUT. Absolutely.

JESSIE. But you didn't see any of his faults at first?

ANGELA. But I've told you that I did. All of them. Only they didn't seem to matter. It was as if they belonged to some other person.

JESSIE. Because you were a bit cracked?

ANGELA. That's what Doctor Macadam seems to think.

LADY DODD. I think it's all summed up by Lord Tennyson when he says that a friend should bear a friend's infirmities. And if you've got to bear a friend's infirmities, how much more ought you to bear a husband's? It's all a matter of give and take.

PADRE. Very true, and excellently put. And now perhaps we may sum up the discussion by saying that marriage is a very good idea indeed if we are prepared to give and take as Lady Dodd says.

MUTCH. But not if it's all on one side.

PADRE. Of course it mustn't be all on one side. I think Lady Dodd made that quite clear.

MUTCH. But it *is* all on one side. I mean to say, what the devil?

[*He stands up and begins to thump the table with his fist to emphasise the points he imagines he is making.*

I mean to say you don't know these people as I do. I mean I've known Angela for fifteen years and George for nearly forty, and I mean to say he's a decent enough fellow and all that sort of thing, but he's bone lazy and bone selfish, and as conceited as a peacock with three tails; though what he's got to be conceited about I don't know, though it's partly her fault of course. I mean, after all, she's got a personality of her own, and what the hell . . . I mean to say, the point is this . . . of course I can't say anything, for some reason or other nobody's supposed to say anything about things like that until the damage is done. But it *is* done. And there's somebody had her whole life spoilt by the bone-headed conceit and stupidity of a little twirp like that; but it's high time someone told him, and I don't care if he knows it.

[*He sits down abruptly.*]

PADRE. The Professor is of the opinion that both partners must be prepared to make some sacrifice, that there must be some give and take, so we'll pass on to the next question.

PROUT. I beg your pardon, we'll do nothing of the kind. This man has had the impudence to come in and out of my house like a tame lap-dog and pretend to be my friend, and now he stands up at a public meeting and insults me in intolerable terms. I want to know what he means by it, if he's capable of stringing a couple of intelligible sentences together.

PADRE. I think you can settle that on a more suitable occasion.

PROUT. No, I insist. He's either said too much or too little. He's got to stand up there and tell us what the devil he means.

MUTCH. I should think I've made my meaning clear enough. I've called you a selfish, conceited, bone-headed twirp, and I mean it. You are one.

PROUT. And what am I supposed to do now? Fight you? You know damn well I can't fight you. You'll hear from my solicitor.

MUTCH. He's my solicitor too. He'll tell you not to be a damn fool. Upon my Sam, I don't know how she sticks him.

PROUT. You keep my wife out of this.

ANGELA. But it's true, George. You are very difficult.

PROUT. That's right. You turn on me now. A minute ago you were rolling your eyes up to heaven and telling the British Navy, Army and Air Force how much you loved me, but it's just like you. I'm not surprised. You insist on being treated like a rational being and at the same time claim the right to behave like a spoilt child. I forgot your birthday three weeks ago and you sulked for ten days. How can I make a comrade and friend and partner out of a creature like that?

MUTCH. I should begin by trying to behave like a gentleman.

PROUT. I suppose you call your behaviour gentlemanly.

MUTCH. I only discuss terms with people who know what they mean.

ANGELA. Oh, stop. I can't bear this.

LADY DODD. Well, to tell you the truth, it's getting a little too much for me.

PADRE. I'm not in the least surprised. Gentlemen, you must either behave yourselves in a civilised fashion, or leave this platform.

MUTCH. Certainly I'll leave this platform, and I'll take Mrs. Prout with me.

PROUT. You'll do nothing of the sort.

MUTCH. Who's going to stop me?

PROUT. I am. (*To* ANGELA.) Are you going to sit there and hear me insulted? I can't imagine a woman with a spark of spirit sitting still and hearing her husband insulted.

LADY DODD. Oh, can't you, Mr. Prout? It's one of the few pleasures we poor women have.

ANGELA. If we're talking about insults, I've been steadily insulted ever since this thing began, and by you, George. And I may tell you I've had about enough of it. You can go on washing our dirty linen in public as long as the Padre will let you. I'm going with Jimmy.

PROUT. I forbid you to do anything of the sort. Why should you? Is he your lover, or what?

ANGELA. Yes, he is. I mean he is—in a way. I mean he is.

[*A short silence.*

PROUT. Do you mean to say this has been going on under my very nose?

MUTCH. Nothing's been going on under your very nose. Don't be silly.

PROUT. I beg your pardon, Professor Mutch. My wife has just stated in the clearest possible terms that she has been deceiving me with you. You set great store by your gentility. Do you accuse my wife of telling lies?

ANGELA. But it isn't what you think it means, George. It isn't at all, honestly.

PROUT. What *do* you mean then? At least I am entitled to an explanation.

ANGELA. Of course, Jimmy and I are very fond of one another—but not in that way.

PROUT. May I ask what you mean by " that way "?

PADRE. No, sir. You certainly may not.

> [*The whole battery of stage-effects is suddenly turned on.*
> *Thunder, rain, lightning. In the pandemonium, the*
> *startled* BRAINS TRUST *sits down and looks at itself*
> *in a dazed sort of way.*

> [*The tumult dies, except for the sound of galloping*
> *horses' hooves dying in the distance.*

JESSIE. When did you begin to feel that way about the Professor, Mrs. Prout?

PADRE. Stop a bit. I don't understand. Who's monkeying about with the light and effects?

JESSIE. Never mind, sir, please sir. Please sit still. I'll tell you later.

PADRE (*severely*). Do you know I have a strong suspicion, Private Killigrew. . . .

PROUT (*rising*). I said that when I married I would marry the perfect woman or die a bachelor. I was ugly. I was poor, but an artist can marry anybody he likes. A wise man told

[60]

me that and I believed him. I was determined to marry a woman who was graceful and beautiful, without blemish, but curiously touched by humanity that she might escape the horror of perfection. I could hear only her voice. It would sound, I thought, like bees on the clover, like quick accidental waterfalls, like the lower notes of the skylark, like the song of the thrush. A voice full of sympathy, but not impertinent sympathy. And talking good sense. And talking good English. And not trying to be clever. The woman would have a personality strong and individual but ready to blend with other personalities, to warm and illuminate them. I knew her. I could hear her. But I could not see her. All I knew was that she would be a surprise. Dark? Fair? It was nothing to me. Height? As high as my heart. But beautiful she must be, and honest and gentle and strong. And look what I married! That!

> [*He walks out abruptly. The* BRAINS TRUST *sit looking at each other in a stunned silence which is broken by* JESSIE.

JESSIE. He didn't want much, did he?

ANGELA. I must go to him. He's so impulsive. The Lord knows what he'll do. He might do anything.

> [*She gets up hurriedly.*

PADRE. I'll meet you outside in two minutes.

LADY DODD. I'll drive you back. We'll catch up with him on the road.

ANGELA. Thank you, Lady Dodd—could we go now?

LADY DODD. Yes, yes. I'm perfectly certain it will be all right.

> [EXIT ANGELA *and* LADY DODD *followed vaguely by* MUTCH.

PADRE. Ladies and gentlemen, I think I'm safe in saying that the Brains Trust is of the opinion that Holy Matrimony is not . . . is hardly a topic for discussion before a mixed

E

audience, so we had better draw these proceedings to a close.

JESSIE. Let down the tabs, Walter.

PADRE. What's this ? Walter ? What Walter ? Where's Walter ?

JESSIE. I wangled him out of the hospital. He wanted to hear the Brains Trust. O.K., Walter.

> [*Curtains draw together and* PADRE *gets entangled with them and eventually appears in front.*

PADRE. Ah ! There you are, ladies and gentlemen. Just before I rush off to see what I can do about this most un-unfortunate *contretemps*, I have to tell you that tomorrow night ENSA is presenting on this stage, Mr. Pete Schacht and his Jiving Strawberries.

> [EXIT PADRE. *The house lights remain out and the orchestra, if any, plays to denote the passage of half an hour.*

END OF SCENE I, ACT III.

ACT III

SCENE II

[As soon as it is humanly possible, the Curtain goes up on the Prouts' Studio. It is completely dark and there is silence for a moment till the purr of a very good motor car is heard, and shortly after somebody turns the key in the door, and ANGELA, LADY DODD, MUTCH *and the* PADRE ENTER, *guided by the Padre's electric torch.*]

MUTCH. Half a jiffy; I'll put on the light. Where the devil is it?

*[*ANGELA *switches on the light.*]

Oh good, I never could find switches.

PADRE. I'm certain it's going to be quite all right.

LADY DODD. So am I. I'm never wrong about these things.

*[*ANGELA *has been busy about the fireplace. She stands up suddenly.*]

ANGELA. Do you think he could have got here before us?

PADRE. He could quite easily if he caught the last bus. That puncture held us up twenty minutes, and we didn't pass it on the road. .

ANGELA. Jimmy, the rat poison!

*[*SHE *runs out, followed by* MUTCH.]

PADRE. Oh dear, perhaps I'd better go too. Excuse me a minute, Lady Dodd.

*[*EXIT PADRE.]

*[*LADY DODD *dusts a seat carefully and sits down, looking round her with some distaste and some curiosity.*

RE-ENTER ANGELA *quickly, followed by the two men. She carries a tin of rat poison.*]

[63]

ANGELA. Well, that's all right, thank God ! The tin hasn't been opened.

LADY DODD. Well, that's a blessing anyway. I don't approve of rat poison. I'm told the poor little things suffer terribly.

ANGELA. Perhaps he's in his room.

[*Noise.*

I'll go to him.

PADRE. No ; perhaps it would be better if Mr. Mutch and I went. Or perhaps it would be better if Professor Mutch didn't go. One never knows exactly how people feel about these things.

MUTCH. I could show you where his room is.

PADRE. Splendid, splendid. Well, come along ; and be quite calm, Mrs. Prout. I'm perfectly certain it's going to turn out all right.

[EXEUNT PADRE *and* MUTCH.

ANGELA. I hope it's all right. He's so very impulsive.

LADY DODD. I think we can leave him to Mr. Paris. Mr. Paris is wonderful. I did admire the way he took complete control of the situation. He even wanted to bring the Medical Officer. It's a pity the poor fellow was so tipsy, and I must say I hadn't much confidence in that old Dr. Macadam. He's quite out of date. I only have him for the servants.

ANGELA. Do you think we'll need a doctor ?

LADY DODD. No, of course we won't. People don't need doctors if they lead ordinary, simple, clean, healthy lives.

ANGELA. But George doesn't lead an ordinary simple, clean, healthy life. And anyhow that's not the point. He may have done something awful.

LADY DODD. Nonsense ! He seemed to me a very sensible cultivated kind of man—in a way. A nice, quiet, well-bred type.

PROUT (*without*). Will you get to hell out of here and mind your own business ?

[64]

PADRE (*without*). But I say, look here, Mr. Prout. Do be sensible.

[ENTER PROUT *in a rage followed by the* PADRE *and* MUTCH.

PADRE. But look here, Mr. Prout—really !

PROUT. I'm not going to have any bloody old woman interfering in my private affairs. Oh, hullo, Lady Dodd, I didn't notice you.

LADY DODD. Good evening, Mr. Prout. You're here, after all. We were very anxious about you ; and you mustn't call me an old woman. It isn't civil, and it isn't true.

PROUT. It wasn't calling you an old woman—I didn't know you were here. I was calling this dog-collared nosey parker an old woman.

MUTCH. Shut up, George, will you ? You're making a damned fool of yourself.

PROUT. And no doubt you're a damned good judge.

ANGELA. George, are you all right ?

PROUT. Of course I'm all right. Who wouldn't be all right after having his private life dragged through the gutter in front of a lot of gaping babboons ? A most stimulating and delightful experience.

ANGELA. Well, it was all your fault. You began it.

PROUT. *My* fault ? *I* began it. Who was it started these damned private theatricals ?

ANGELA. You did.

PROUT. I did ? You did. Split my windpipe, I have my faults but I'm not a damned exhibitionist like you. And as for Jimmy. . . .

MUTCH. I chipped in when I thought you were going too far.

PROUT. You mean you lost your temper—in front of all those people.

MUTCH. I didn't ; anyhow how could anyone keep his temper ?

ANGELA. It all seemed to come over me somehow.

[65]

PROUT. It's always coming over you.

MUTCH. Shut up, you.

PROUT. Why should I ?

PADRE. Now, now, now, now. This isn't very helpful.

PROUT (*turning on him*). And now thank you for your visit, your reverence, and will you be good enough to take yourself out of here and leave me to the peace of my family circle ?

PADRE. I shall do nothing of the sort. Jessie's bringing round a jeep for me presently ; but until she comes I'm going to do my best to get you into a better frame of mind.

PROUT. Even at the risk of being kicked out.

PADRE. I'm afraid you can't do that very well. You see I happen to be. . . .

PROUT. I know, I know. The ex-middle-weight champion of the Monastery, but look out.

LADY DODD. This is quite, quite ridiculous. When any of my friends had trouble with their wives, they often wanted to horsewhip the other fellow or shoot him or something. They never thought of kicking the vicar.

PROUT. No doubt you're right, but if he doesn't clear out I'll send for the police. Or I'll set Jimmy on him. He likes brawling and mauling and punching people on the nose.

ANGELA. Jimmy won't do anything of the sort.

PADRE. There isn't going to be any punching on the nose. Do let's sit down and behave like civilised beings.

PROUT. You're not going to clear out ?

PADRE. No.

PROUT. Then I will.

MUTCH. Chuck it, George, for God's sake. We've got to get this straight.

PROUT. I know we have, but what's he got to do with it ?

MUTCH. I don't know ; but he seems to be able to keep his head, and—well—I mean to say, the rest of us are hardly a picture of sound commonsense.

LADY DODD. The professor is perfectly right. Let's all have a cosy chat. I've always found it doesn't lead anywhere, but it lets off steam, and you sometimes hear the most fright-fully interesting things. Come along, Mrs. Prout, make your husband behave himself.

ANGELA. I don't seem to have any influence over him at all.

LADY DODD. Well, in that case, you'd better do as I tell you, Mr. Prout. Sit beside me.

[ALL *sit.* PROUT *beside* LADY DODD, MUTCH *beside* ANGELA, *and the* PADRE *a little apart.*

LADY DODD. Well, now. The three of you have got your-selves into a mess, and you have been silly enough not to keep quiet about it. In fact, I never saw any three people quite so silly about an ordinary little domestic upset. If people started pulling the roof down every time somebody took a fancy to another man's wife there wouldn't be a single good family left in Britain. Now, Mr. Paris, tell them what you think, and don't be afraid.

PADRE. It all seems perfectly simple to me.

PROUT. As the bomb said when it landed on the Art Gallery.

LADY DODD. Please don't interrupt, Mr. Prout.

PADRE. We all have absurd inclinations and we don't always behave very wisely, but there's one thing we owe to our self-respect and that is to play the game.

MUTCH. What game ?

PADRE. You're a public schoolboy. You should know what playing the game means. We must have some kind of standards, and I don't know of any better than the good old sporting standards of the New Testament.

MUTCH. Well—I mean to say—good gracious—for heaven's sake. . . !

PADRE. If only you fellows would read your Bibles you would understand exactly what I mean by "playing the game." Professor Mutch, I must be absolutely frank with you. You are not playing the game.

PROUT. Hear, hear.

[67]

PADRE. You seem to me to have deliberately set yourself to break up the family life of two of your friends. That is what I mean by not playing the game.

MUTCH. Do you know anything about their family life?

PADRE. Not a great deal. But family life is family life all the world over.

MUTCH. If that means that family life is the same all the world over, I mean to say, for heaven's sake! It isn't the same in two semi-detached villas. It certainly isn't the same in Aberdeen and Timbuctoo.

PADRE. It is essentially the same in Aberdeen and Timbuctoo. It is based on a solemn contract between a man and a woman. If you break the contract the whole system falls down.

MUTCH. Yes, but I mean to say, what's the basis of the contract? I mean to say, the point is, it's out of date. It was framed to meet the needs of a primitive society nearly two thousand years ago.

PADRE. It's a good deal older than that and we're still a primitive society.

ANGELA. Oh, but Padre—we are *not* a primitive society. At least not *our* kind of people. We know more about ourselves. I don't mind telling you I've been psycho-analysed three times. I mean really *deep* psycho-analysis, and I ought to know what I'm talking about.

LADY DODD. Well, I don't know. You remember that little girl who was eating apples and fiddling with the light? She put a question to the Brains Trust and you tried to help her out of her difficulty, and all you did was to get yourselves into the most outrageous mess.

PADRE. That's very interesting. But perhaps I'd better say this—Professor Mutch has behaved very badly, and Mrs. Prout has exercised very little self-control. I am quite clear in my mind about that. If Mr. and Mrs. Prout have stuck it for fifteen years they can stick it for another twenty-five, and they've just jolly well got to. The Professor ought to go and get married and settle down. It would do him a world of good.

LADY DODD. I quite agree.

MUTCH. It's not so easy as all that.

ANGELA. It isn't by any means.

MUTCH. I'm sorry for George. He can't help it. I mean to say, he's quite a decent fellow, but he and Angela aren't suited to one another. You saw for yourselves that it was a pure accident that they got married at all. I mean to say, there was no reason—no foresight in it. The result has been fifteen years of pure undiluted hell, I mean to say, not for Angela alone, but for George too. I mean to say, I've known them nearly all my life, and I've been very worried about it. And it was really worrying about that that gave me this sort of what-you-may-call-it—*fixation* I've got for Angela. God knows I don't want to bust up George's arrangements, to say nothing of my own, but I really think the best way would be for me to take over the responsibility for Angela and leave George to find someone more suitable. What do you think? Eh?

PADRE. Mrs. Prout, would you say that your married life for fifteen years had been pure, undiluted hell?

ANGELA. Yes, on the whole I would.

PADRE. What?

ANGELA. And it won't be any better after this. George was difficult enough to get on with as he was without being all torn up with jealousy and suspicion.

PADRE. But surely Mr. Prout would be reasonable.

ANGELA. He might be, but I've never known him try to be. Just look at him sitting there—sulking. Does he look like a reasonable man?

> [PROUT *does not look like a reasonable man. He is sitting with his arms folded in a state of obstinate gloom, staring straight in front of him.*

PADRE. Mr. Prout, if your wife promises never to see

[69]

Professor Mutch again, will you forgive and forget and let bygones be bygones?

ANGELA.   But I'm not going to promise any such thing. Jimmy's the only thing that's made life bearable for me. If I stay on with George and darn his socks and cook his meals he's just got to lump it.

PADRE.   But that would never do.

LADY DODD.   Of course not.

ANGELA.   Then we've just got to go away together. George can divorce me if he likes.

MUTCH.   Hold on a minute. I hardly think, if you follow me, we ought to make up our minds quite so precipitately. I mean to say, my housekeeper has got a terrible antipathy to children. She had one illegitimate child that grew up and stole all her savings.

LADY DODD.   But couldn't you get rid of her?

MUTCH.   I've tried to get rid of her for over twenty years. She wouldn't mind Angela—at least I don't think so—but she couldn't stand the children.

ANGELA.   You might have had the decency to tell me that before.

MUTCH.   I did tell you.

ANGELA.   No, you didn't. Not in so many words. Of course if you prefer your housekeeper to me. . . .

MUTCH.   But I don't, my darling. Only I can't afford to pension her and she's too old to get another job.

ANGELA.   I think if I'm prepared to break up my domestic arrangements you might go a little way in breaking up yours.

MUTCH.   But I've explained, darling. I mean to say, after all, whatever way you look at it, the point is. . . .

ANGELA.   Don't you love me?

MUTCH.   I love you with my whole soul.

ANGELA.   And I love you too. Don't you see we've got to do something about it?

MUTCH.   Yes. But why rush things? After all, we're proposing to take a terrific step. We've got to examine it from every angle.

[70]

ANGELA (*in tears*) I'm sick of examining angles.

PADRE. Look here, Mrs. Prout; pull yourself together. You've got to make a clean break. You've simply got to. There's nothing else for it. I'll talk to Mr. Prout tomorrow when he's in a better state of mind.

PROUT. You will not.

PADRE. Now, now, come, come.

PROUT. I'm damned if I'll come, come.   Mind your own business.

PADRE. But this is my business.

LADY DODD. Of course it is, Mr. Prout. Mr. Paris's business is to make people good, and you have all been very naughty indeed.

PROUT. I've been nothing of the sort.

MUTCH. Yes, you have, George. It would never have happened if it hadn't been for you.

PROUT. The cat wouldn't have stolen the milk if it hadn't been for the milkman or the dairymaid and the cow—and the parish bull, if it comes to that. I prefer to blame the cat.

MUTCH. If you had treated Angela properly. . . .

ANGELA. Oh, it wasn't that, it wasn't that at all.

PROUT. Thank you for those few nuts.

MUTCH. Well, why then. . . .? I mean to say, I always thought—— For goodness' sake! I mean to say, what did start it?

ANGELA. It wasn't George anyway. I never thought very much of him, but I was terribly fond of him and I knew he couldn't help being a bully and a brute sometimes. All artists are neurotics. They wouldn't be artists if they weren't. They'd settle down and do some honest work. I knew what I was doing when I married George, and I knew how to put up with him. I could even manage him a bit. It wasn't that at all.

MUTCH. What was it then?

ANGELA. I don't know. People who are in love get to be in love with love. And in the long, long times when George was somewhere else, or with his head all muffled in the

[71]

clouds, absorbed in his painting, I felt restless and silly and hungry. I thought it was sympathy I wanted, but it was love I wanted. People don't think of that when they blame people.

LADY DODD. That's very true.

PADRE. Well, it is a sort of an excuse ; but I must say I can't find any excuse for Professor Mutch's conduct. I can only call it by a very disagreeable name indeed : philandering.

LADY DODD. Have you got an excuse, Mr. Mutch ?

MUTCH. Well, is it a matter for excuses ? I mean to say, it seems to me on the face of it that situations like this arise in a sort of a way from a variety of causes and that only a very small percentage of these causes are in any way under our control, if I may put it that way. What I mean to say is this. . . .

PROUT. Shut up !

MUTCH. Eh ?

PROUT. Shut up ! You never could explain anything. I'll explain it for you if you like.

MUTCH. But you're biassed.

PROUT (*He turns to* LADY DODD, *markedly ignoring the* PADRE). Lady Dodd, there's a certain type of man who is doomed to be a stray dog, and you'll agree, I think, that stray dogs are very pathetic.

LADY DODD. Of course they are. They're the saddest things in the whole world.

PROUT. Very well, then. Jimmy's a stray dog. If anybody's kind to him and gives him a bone and a cookhouse fire to sit at, he goes all maudlin. He goes off his head. He can bark and snarl all the way down the street. He can bite the children who try to tie tin cans to his tail . . . did you ever hear him lecturing to his students ? You'd be amazed.

LADY DODD. No.

PROUT. A famished wolf at bay has nothing on Jimmy lecturing to his students. . . . Very well then. We gave him a fireside, and some carbolic soap to get rid of his fleas, and got all his crazy devotion in return. The trouble is that no woman can be trusted with a dog.

LADY DODD. Oh, what nonsense!

PROUT. No, but it's true. They're not content with taking the brute for a run and feeding it and throwing sticks for it, and teaching it a few self-respecting tricks. They set to work and steadily undermine its morale until it's a cringing nervous little horror. It's not the dog's fault. They talk baby talk to it. They let it slobber all over their faces. They take it to bed with them at night.

[*A loud knock on the door is heard.*

ANGELA. Answer that, Jimmy, will you.   (*To* PROUT.) You're a low despicable cad.

PADRE. Yes.

LADY DODD. I almost agree with you.

MUTCH (*at the door*). Oh, here's Jessie. Shall I bring her in?

PROUT. Bring in the Navy, the Army, the Royal Air Force and the Home Guard. What the hell does it matter?

[ENTER JESSIE.

(*To* JESSIE.) Come along in.

JESSIE. I've brought the car round, sir.

PADRE. Thank you, Jessie.

JESSIE. I hope you don't mind, sir—I've brought Walter too.

PROUT. Bring him in. No doubt he's passionately interested in our private affairs.

JESSIE (*to* PADRE). Is that all right, sir?

PADRE. Is what all right?

JESSIE. Can I bring Walter in?

MUTCH. I say, this is a bit thick.

PROUT. You shut up. I may be a blooming cuckold but I'm still master of this house. Bring him in.

JESSIE. Okey-doke.

[EXIT JESSIE.

PROUT. We're supposed to be helping this young couple to solve their problems. We've made a fine mess of it. I

[73]

want them to see where people land themselves by being too damned clever.

> [ENTER JESSIE *and* WALTER. *He is a self-possessed, rather loutish young man in soiled hospital blues. He holds a spanner in his hand, but stands smartly to attention.*

JESSIE. This is Walter. He can stand easy, can't he?

PADRE. Yes, yes.

> [WALTER *stands very easy indeed.*

ANGELA. Won't you sit down?

> [MUTCH *brings a chair for* WALTER, *who sits down.*

WALTER. Ta.

JESSIE. I hope it's all right me bringing Walter. He told the Provo' Sergeant he had to bring back three lantern slides.

PADRE. What lantern slides?

JESSIE. Well, there aren't any; but the Provo' Sergeant couldn't be expected to know that. (*Then brightly.*) Well? Have they settled everything all right?

PADRE. Half of these problems arise just because people think too much about them. If more people took a cold bath and a sharp walk before breakfast, there would be less of this sort of thing. Now look here, all of you. The only way out of this is for you three to make some sort of sacrifice.

MUTCH. Why?

PADRE. It's the only way to get back your self-respect.

MUTCH. But we've never lost it. I've got a great respect for myself.

PADRE. I'm sorry to hear it.

MUTCH. You want me to give up. . . . By the way you *are* rather a clever fellow George — I never argue by analogy; but you hit the nail on the head—I am a bit of a lost dog. . . . You want me to give up the only patch of happiness I've ever found in my poor drab scholar's life. You want Angela to give up the only thing that makes the life of a woman and a poet, worth living. You want George to give up his life's work. I mean to say, why not ask us to turn on the gas and be done with it. I mean to say, do try to be a little reasonable.

PADRE. But it can't go on, on this footing.

PROUT. It certainly damn well can't.

LADY DODD. I think we should all go home to bed.

PADRE. No, I'm sorry. We can't leave it this way.

PROUT. You can all go home as far as I'm concerned—and that applies to Jimmy too. He's certainly not going to stay here. And he can take Angela with him if he likes.

MUTCH. Where the devil can I take Angela at this time of night? I've nowhere to go myself if it comes to that.

PROUT. Fat lot I care.

ANGELA. George, you must be sensible.

PROUT. Sensible!

JESSIE. Please, may I say something?

PROUT. Go on, go on.

JESSIE. I think we should ask Walter what he thinks.

PADRE. Really, Jessie, behave yourself.

WALTER. Gercher!

JESSIE. No, honestly. Walter looks a bit soft, but he's all there, all right. What do you think they ought to do, Walter?

WALTER. Well, I don't know all the facts, but when you've got a lot of blokes and judies with too much time on their hands, well, it stands to reason you get a bit of square-pushing. Well, most times it don't do no harm. It all depends how bad you've got it. Well, say a gent gets sweet on another gent's judy, the gent what owns the judy he's got two or three things he can do. He can go about yapping and bellyaching; he can clock the other guy one and give his judy something to remember. But that don't do much good in my experience. If he licks the other guy, it's the other guy the judy's sorry for. If the other guy licks him the judy thinks he's a poor enough piece of cheese. The best way in my experience is to sit down over a pint of wallop and say—" Here, chum, what about it? There's plenty of other judies in the world, yapping about and leaving their hair combing's all over the place. What do you want to come messing around my judy for? She takes a bit of getting used to—I warn you, and I got used to her. Anyhow," you says, " love and that's all very well, but you've got your life to live. If you look at it reasonable, judies is things that most blokes can do with in moderation. There's things you've got to do. You've got to eat and you've got to sleep, but you ain't got to go running after other blokes' judies. I've seen the time I'd have give the most wonderful judy in the world for a plate of bully and a slice of bread and marge. So have a bit of sense, chum. And what about one for the road?" That's what I'd say if I was in his place. Anyways, I think I would. You never know. . . .

JESSIE. That's right. Walter's right. You haven't got it as bad as all that, Mrs. Prout, and the Professor certainly hasn't. You'll get over it all right, if you mark time for a bit, and Mr. Prout doesn't go on whacking it up like a scene in the pictures.

ANGELA. I like that. I like that very much. You've settled it all, haven't you? But what about you and Walter?

JESSIE. Oh, that's all right.

ANGELA. Is it? Aren't you in love with the Padre?

WALTER. What?

JESSIE. Amn't I what?

ANGELA. That was your whole difficulty, wasn't it?

PADRE. Good gracious me, what a terrible thing to say! Really, Mrs. Prout, you ought to know better.

JESSIE. The Padre's a very nice gentleman, but nobody's going to fall in love with him; not without their feeling specially holy or something.

WALTER. Ah!

JESSIE. Besides you've done me a bit of good on the Brains Trust tonight. I'm going to marry someone practical. Are you ready to go, sir?

PADRE. Well, after Mrs. Prout's extraordinary remark, I don't think there's anything else to do. I hope, Lady Dodd, you didn't think for a moment . . . .

[76]

[PADRE *picks up his hat with braces.* LADY DODD *turns to speak to him with her hand out.* PADRE *tries to give braces to* WALTER, *who half backs away.* PADRE *looks to see if his own braces have come off. Drops them as if they were a snake.*

PADRE (*under his breath*).   For God's sake let me get out of here.

[EXIT

PROUT.   In love with the padre?

ANGELA.   Shut up.

PROUT (*to* MUTCH).   In love with the padre!

[EXEUNT JESSIE, WALTER *and the* PADRE *all murmuring "Goodnight."*

[LADY DODD *makes ready to depart.*

LADY DODD.   And now, Professor, if you've got a tooth-brush and a suit of pyjamas I think you had better come along to the Hall for tonight, and I don't mind telling you that we have one or two quite nice firesides to sit at, and perhaps even a bone or two.   And I'm very fond of stray dogs.

MUTCH.   Well, I mean to say, it's most terribly good of you.

PROUT.   No, no, he'd better stay here.

ANGELA.   No, Jimmy.   You'd better go.   Go now.   Your bag's packed already and I'll push in your pyjamas.   You left them in the bathroom.

[MUTCH *opens the door for her.*

MUTCH.   I don't know.   I feel a bit guilty.

ANGELA.   You needn't.   Only you'd better get into the car now and not keep Lady Dodd waiting.

MUTCH.   But what are you going to do?

ANGELA.   I'm going to town next week to have my hair done in rows of tight little lumps like iron filings.   I'll feel all right then.

[EXIT ANGELA.

[LADY DODD *prepares to depart.*

F   [77]

LADY DODD. Well, now, Mr. Prout, perhaps your charming wife will forgive us if we take her at her word. You'll say goodbye to her for me, won't you? Come along, Professor.

PROUT. Oh, yes; all right. Thank you. Good-bye.

[EXIT LADY DODD.

PROUT. Oh, by the way, Jimmy.

MUTCH. Eh?

PROUT. Your train doesn't go till 2.45. I wish you'd look in some time in the course of the morning. I want to ask your advice about those spring onions.

MUTCH. Why . . . yes, of course; certainly. Yes, naturally. But I mean to say, I've been thinking it over and you were absolutely right, old boy. I mean to say, they wouldn't leave them above ground unless they had some reason for it and probably a very good reason too.

PROUT. No, that's very true.

[RE-ENTER ANGELA *with bag.*

ANGELA. Are you still here? Take this and clear out.

MUTCH. Oh, yes, righto. Thank you, Well, good-bye, then.

ANGELA. Get out.

[EXIT MUTCH.

PROUT. I don't think you ought to have talked to Jimmy like that.

ANGELA. I nearly threw the bag at him.

PROUT. No doubt. But he's a sensitive sort of fellow and you were damned rude.

ANGELA. My God! . . . Oh, what's the use? George, why must you leave braces lying about all over the place? You know you never wear them.

PROUT. I hardly think this is a time to be talking about braces.

ANGELA. No, perhaps not.

(SHE *lifts some stockings off the easel. Then sits on divan beside* PROUT *and begins to darn a sock.*

PROUT. Oh, Lord, this place is a positive dog's breakfast.

ANGELA. I thought you liked it that way.

PROUT. Yes, I do. And somehow we always seem to be able to find things. There's one thing I want, though.

ANGELA. There isn't a drop in the house.

PROUT. What about a cup of tea ?

ANGELA. I'll put the kettle on.

PROUT. No ; I'll put the kettle on.

> [HE EXITS. *As this is the first time for years that he has ever done a spontaneously civil action* ANGELA *registers first astonishment, then delight, and darns the sock with fresh gusto.*

CURTAIN.

END OF THE PLAY